HONEST TALK
A New Perspective on
Talking to Your Kids About Sex

by John W Fort

WWW.BEBROKEN.COM

HONEST TALK

Be Broken, Garden Ridge, TX 78266
www.bebroken.com
Copyright © 2019 by Be Broken

Unless otherwise indicated, Scripture quotations are taken from the New American Standard Bible. Copyright © 1960, 1962, 1963, 1968, 1971, 1972, 1973, 1975, 1977, 1995 by The Lockman Foundation. Used by permission.

Scripture quotations marked NIV are taken from THE HOLY BIBLE, NEW INTERNATIONAL VERSION®, NIV® Copyright © 1973, 1978, 1984, 2011 by Biblica, Inc.® Used by permission. All rights reserved worldwide.

Cover Design: Sydney Fort
Illustrations: Sydney Fort & Elliot Elison

ISBN: 9781796685800

Printed in The United States of America

CONTENTS

SPECIAL THANKS

This book reflects far more than my personal knowledge. I owe a very special thanks to Dr. John Thorington, Ann Martin, Geremy Keeton, Dr. Juli Slattery, and Jay Stringer for lending your counseling expertise to this project. I dare not take credit without acknowledging your help, especially with the more difficult topics addressed in these pages.

PART ONE
Preparing Ourselves

1

The Role of the Parent

You care deeply about your child. If you did not, you would not be reading this book. You want them to avoid the emotional and relational pain that come with sexual brokenness, such as compulsive pornography use or sexual promiscuity. Hopefully, you also wish for them to one-day experience sexual bliss within marital union. These are things a loving parent wants for their child.

You may also desire for your child to experience a relationship with God that brings them peace and a sense of fulfillment. Perhaps a hope that they will know what it is like to be filled with the wisdom of the Holy Spirit and experience His love. A longing that your child will enter into the saving grace of Jesus and know His forgiveness and the freedom that comes with it. These are also things a loving parent would want for their children.

In the ideal scenario a child would learn to unite their sexuality and spirituality under the grace and guidance of their heavenly Father. If we are honest, and honesty is a core concept of this book, we admit that this does not happen very often.

I need you to hear this next thought very clearly. A child can grow up devoid of most forms of sexual brokenness and still not know God. A child can also accept Christ at a young age and be fully forgiven yet grow up completely enmeshed in sexual brokenness. A child who is saved, prays daily, reads their Bible daily, and attends church and youth services every single week, is in no way immune to pornography, sexual fantasy, masturbation, or sexual promiscuity. Jesus may save your child's soul, but we as parents have a God-given responsibility to mentor them toward sexual wholeness.

Train up a child in the way he should go.
Even when he is old he will not depart from it.[1]
—King Solomon

Fathers, do not exasperate your children; instead,
bring them up in the training and instruction of the Lord[2].
—The Apostle Paul

A child may love God but worry that God is mad at them because they looked at pornography when a friend showed it to them. An adolescent may pray but not know how to, or that they even should, ask God what to do with their sexual feelings. They need our help sorting out what to do with God and sexuality.

A Personal Story

This book is not my story, but my story helps illustrate this point. I grew up in a Christian home. My family was all in on the Christian bandwagon. My father was a pastor and became a denominational leader by the time I was seven. He taught me more about the true nature of God than any Bible study, theological book, sermon or class. I watched and emulated his genuine relationship with his heavenly Father. My father is the primary reason I have a relationship with God and the reason I pursue God to greater depths even today.

My father told me nothing about sex. I mean absolutely nothing, not even a "birds and the bees" talk. He is passed now so I cannot ask but I have no idea what struggles he may have had with sexual fantasy, masturbation or pornography. I do not know if he was a

---

[1] Proverbs 22:6 (NASB)
[2] Ephesians 6:4 (NIV)

3

virgin on his wedding night. I have no idea what internal struggles he might have had trying to understand what to do with his sexuality as a teenager.

I was left to navigate sexuality on my own. When I was young, I could not talk to God about times that I had seen pornography. I was too ashamed. When I was a teenager, I prayed and begged God to take away my desire to do sexually unhealthy things, but God did not do that. I prayed and prayed, but my sexuality only became more impulsive, not godlier. By age fifteen I was completely confused about the apparent contradiction between what my church said about God's power to conquer sin and my personal experience. With no one to mentor me, I came to an unfortunate conclusion: Either God was not powerful enough to help me with sexual temptation or I had sinned so badly that He didn't want to help me any more. My reaction was to cling to God, desperately hoping He would change His mind and love me enough to help me. Meanwhile, my sexuality continued to spiral out of control.

Pause & Reflect

It is good to pause now to reflect on how you are reacting to what we are learning. Take a moment to do just that.

1. How are you feeling right now? Stop reading for a moment and pay attention what is going on inside you.
2. What emotions are rising up within you? Are those emotions coming from something that happened in your past or a sense of protection for your own children?
3. When you read this story and think of your children, what thoughts go through your mind?

You Are Not My Father

You are not like the parents who remain silent. You invested your own money in order to be more prepared to help your children. You are spending your free time to read a parenting book rather than do something more entertaining. I will strive to entertain, but I can't compete with *The Guardians of the Galaxy*. Yet you choose to keep reading!

You understand that it is not okay to remain silent about sexuality when our children need our help. You know we live in a hypersexual culture that will destroy our children if we do not speak up. The good news is this book aims to make those conversations easier for you.

Where Are We Going?

The goal of this book is to help you guide your children toward a future of sexual fulfillment that is merged with their spirituality and healthy relationships with others. Sexuality is not something separate from the rest of our lives but an integral part of all aspects of who we are. For simplicity we will refer to this sexual, spiritual, and relational ideal as "sexual wholeness" throughout this book.

No human ever achieves perfect sexual wholeness. You are not entirely sexual whole and your children will not be either. Like any other ideal that God designs, none of us ever achieve it on this side of heaven. Instead, we want to move our children and ourselves continually in the direction of sexual wholeness.

Because we as parents have our own journey toward sexual wholeness, the process of helping our children involves inviting them on the journey with us. The older they get the more we are able to share about what we have learned on our journey that may help them on theirs. This is a highly relational process, not a set of rules we hand our children to follow.

You will likely learn things while reading this book that help you on your journey toward sexual wholeness. Depending on the age of your children right now, you may have time to try some ideas out for yourself before telling your children what you have learned. In that case, not only will you be able to give information to your child that comes from this book, but you will also be able to share your own experience trying these ideas for yourself. Sharing your own experience trying ideas and methods is a more effective teacher than reciting what you read.

We are going on a journey; one that you will invite your children onto as they are ready.

Honest About What?

Sexuality is a sensitive subject. So is spirituality if we are honest about what we actually experience with God. It does our children little good to present an unrealistic viewpoint of sex and faith. Doing so will only lead to disappointment and disillusionment in our children. This is what I experienced because adults were not honest with me about God and sex when I was a child. You want something better than that for your child.

When we are honest about sex and about our relationship with God, we can present a realistic picture of what growing up looks like. We may fear that reality paints a messier picture than we want our children to see. However, when we are honest with our children about the realities of sex and spiritual experience, they learn to trust us. They come to know we are telling the truth; which they don't hear many other places.

We want our children to be honest with us about questions they have and things they are exposed to. We cannot help them move toward sexual wholeness otherwise. Our children will not be honest with us, however, unless we are honest with them. This means we will have to share with them parts of our sexual and spiritual story. We will do so at appropriate ages and in appropriate detail.

Safe Honesty

Honesty is powerful. We need to be careful how we utilize that power. We can be responsible with our honesty to ensure it builds up our children rather than damages them.

The purpose of sharing our story with our children is to demonstrate we understand struggles they may be experiencing. This strengthens the bond between us and helps them feel understood. This makes us feel safe to talk to. On the other hand, if we share too many details our story may traumatize them.

For example, we can share general categories of our experiences, such as pornography use, without details of exactly what we saw. We should not share parts of our story that we have not yet shared with our spouse. It is unfair to burden a child with information they feel they must hide from another parent. In telling our story we also want to assure our children that we are not asking for or expecting help from them to fix any current issues we still struggle with. It is okay for a child to know we still have issues we are working on, but they need to feel comfort in knowing we are getting help from outside sources, not them.

We will review these cautions in more detail throughout the book. I will also provide additional guidance to know when and how it is good to share your story with you children.

If you are beginning to feel nervous, there are a few truths that I want you to pay close attention to:

1. Your child is in the right home to discover sexual wholeness.
2. You are the right parent to mentor them.
3. This is not too hard.
4. You can do this.

Parent Challenge

You will get more out of this book if you have someone with whom you can discuss what you're learning. If you're married, we highly recommend that you share your thoughts with your spouse. If you're single, we would recommend that you find another parent to discuss the thoughts you have as you go through this book.

At the end of each chapter we will provide a personal challenge to help you live out what you are learning here.

Here is your first challenge:

Share with your spouse or another adult something your parents did not tell you about sex and how that negatively impacted you.

2

Overcoming Fear

I was afraid to teach almost everything I needed to discuss with my children about sex. I am not the perfect example of a parent being responsible and setting a date to have a needed conversation and seeing it through. I put off conversations I knew I needed to have numerous times. My son told it like this when he was seventeen:

I remember the first time my dad and I started talking about sex. I recall my dad being very nervous, almost embarrassed, talking about it with me. He was scratching the back of his head; he was pacing around a little too much; he just seemed very uneasy and couldn't find what to say. The fear he had about discussing sex isn't abnormal— it's something I feel that all parents experience.[3]

We fear a lot of things related to talking about sex with our children. We are afraid our children will be too embarrassed and won't talk with us. We are afraid we don't know the right words to say. We fear we might put ideas in their heads and stir up unnecessary curiosity about sex. We are afraid we are bad examples

---

[3] Lucas Fort, *Pure Parenting Seminar*, Beaverton, OR (2015)

of sexual wholeness. These are all understandable parental fears and it is okay to talk about them. None of these fears, however, are based in truth.

Our children learn quite easily to be comfortable talking about sex at home. We are the ones who have a hard time with this and we can get over it. You also have this book and will learn how to talk about sex appropriately with your child. As for stirring up curiosity, it is far better for parents to introduce a child to what is out there and prepare them to deal with that information than to wait for them to be exposed to it and not know what to do.

Our Greatest Fear

The greatest fear many parents have is being honest with our children about sex, particularly about our own past. However, in my experience one of the most common reasons parents' attempts to help their children avoid sexual pitfalls fail is because they are *not* willing to be honest with their children about sex. If we want to help our children navigate sexual feelings, the best tool we have is sharing the sexual feelings we had at their age.

I've heard parents say, "That's too personal," or "That feels too invasive to discuss." It is true that we need to be careful not to get too graphic in sharing our story and some details may need to be left out, but that does not mean it is okay to hide things from our children. Your story is the most powerful tool you have in teaching your child about sex.

A common reason many of us fear being honest with our children about our own story is that many of us are ashamed of our past. We fear our children may reject us if they knew what we did at their age or we fear our story sets a bad example. The truth is quite the opposite.

My wife and I both have histories of sexual brokenness in one form or another. Don't take this the wrong way, but we discovered it was helpful that our pasts were so imperfect. The truth we discovered is: all of us have experience, successful or not, with sexual temptation and hurts. The forms temptation comes in may have changed in our children's generation, but the feelings inside have not. We found that our children were more interested in knowing we understood what it felt like to be sexually tempted or curious than that we were a perfect example for them to follow.

When it comes to the pursuit of sexual wholeness, **our failures are what qualify us** to mentor our children. Paul demonstrates this in his letter to Timothy.

> *Christ Jesus came into the world to save sinners—**of whom I am the worst**. But for that very reason I was shown mercy so that in me, the worst of sinners, Christ Jesus might display his immense patience as an example for those who would believe in Him and receive eternal life[4].*
> *—The Apostle Paul*

Paul was personally selected by God to tell the Gentile world about Jesus. God did not choose Paul because he was the best example, but because his past was the worst. Paul could demonstrate hope to those who feared they were not good enough in ways a better example could not.

Your children don't need a perfect example. They need a flawed example that can relate to the struggles they will have. Your story is not shameful. It is hopeful.

An Example of a Parent Being Honest

Let me give you an example of how a parent's story helps a child. I recently spoke with a twenty-year-old young man. He shared how in his teens he developed a very serious problem with pornography and inappropriate sexual behavior with a girlfriend. This young man told me that when he was discovered his father did a very helpful thing. The first thing his father did was to tell him his own story. This included all the sexual things his father had struggled with as a teen. The father shared no graphic details but enough that his son clearly understood what his father had done as a teen; all of it. At that time his father did not share any potential solutions or how it all turned out in the end.

---

4 1 Timothy 1:15–16 (NIV) emphasis added

This young man told me hearing his father share his stories gave him huge relief. He realized at that moment he was not too broken to be loved by his parents or by God. For the first time he felt a sense of hope that he had someone to talk to about sex and maybe his father could help him. That event, just hearing his father's sexual story, became the turning point for this young man to actively engage in his own journey toward sexual wholeness.

Think carefully about what this story demonstrates to us. What was it that truly turned this young man around? It was not reading the Bible. It was not praying. It was not rules, a lecture, consequences or punishment. It was his father's honest story. A lot of work came after, both spiritually and relationally, but the one thing that got his attention was his father's story.

Your child is going to experience some form of sexual brokenness before they reach their adult years. It may be something done to them or something they do. Rather than become alarmed at this, we can simply recognize that all of us, every single parent reading this book, have our own sexual brokenness in one form or another. The greatest comfort you can provide your child very well may be your story of sexual brokenness. That invites them into the journey toward sexual wholeness alongside you.

Parent Challenge

Share with your spouse or another parent what your personal greatest fear is when trying to guide your child toward sexual wholeness. This could be a discussion you know you will need to have with them or something you need to do to protect them but are not sure how to do it.

3

Understanding Sexual Wholeness

It is a mistake for parents to focus on all the ways sexuality can be broken or twisted before presenting the good purpose of sex. The first step in honest talk about sex is to help our children understand what sexual wholeness looks like.

What Sexual Wholeness is Not

Not About Rules

Sexual wholeness is not about following a set of rules. Sexual integrity is the opposite of "anything goes," but focusing on a set of rules about sex completely misses the intention of God's design. More importantly, kids break rules. It's what they do. Focusing on rules is not an effective means of mentoring.

Not About Perfection

There is no such thing as sexual perfection. Even the frequently used phrase "sexual purity" can be misleading. If purity equals perfection, there are and never have been any sexually pure humans.

Every one of us carries scars of sexual brokenness. Scars can come in many forms, including the fear of sex or not enjoying sex. We were designed to enjoy sex! Of course, sexual brokenness can also look like compulsive, self-centered behavior.

Our children will not demonstrate perfection in their sexuality. It is very helpful to them and us not to expect them to be perfect in this area.

Not Only About Sex

Sexual wholeness or integrity or purity encompass much more than a physical act. As we will see there are many other components that must be included in our conversations with our children for them to approach sexual wholeness. It may be a relief for some parents to realize that at least 50% of the important conversations we need to have with our children do not involve anything we typically think of as sexual.

Sexual wholeness includes relational health, spiritual depth, and emotional resilience. Emotional maturity, as we will see, plays an enormous role in sexual wholeness.

Sexual Wholeness is a Journey

Sexual wholeness, above all, is a journey, not a destination. It is moving toward something. It focuses not on what is wrong with our sexuality but what we can do right. It focuses forward, not backward. Sexual wholeness focuses not on the last time we messed up but toward the next time we will live out our sexuality as it was designed to live. On this journey the times we "mess up" become less frequent as we become more whole.

Purity

I want to go back to the phrase "sexual purity," which I mentioned earlier. I actually like that phrase but think there is a more helpful way to think of purity as it relates to sex than we normally hear.

Let us compare sexual purity with pure water. Water never starts out pure in nature. We often call spring water pure, but even spring water is full of microbes and minerals. Even if these happen to be "good microbes and minerals," they still make water impure. Truly pure water is H_2O and nothing else. I dare you to try to find that in nature. You will not. Even raindrops are full of stuff that is not water.

Water is purified through a process—a journey of sorts—that removes everything but the water. Our sexuality is no different. Impurities begin to enter our sexuality at a young age. A sexual joke a friend tells, a character on TV treating someone as a sex object, pornography flashed in the face by a friend with a cell phone. Children are exposed to contamination long before they reach puberty.

There is no need to feel alarmed, however. The culture of Jesus' day was even more highly saturated with inappropriate sex than we have today. Sexual impurity is not something new we suddenly have to deal with. The better news is God has a solution.

Like removing dirt from water we can help remove the impurities that affect our children's sexuality. Sexual purification, integrity, or wholeness is a journey or a process we invite our children into. As they have impurities removed from their sexuality, they move closer to wholeness. None of us are ever completely sexually pure before we reach heaven, but we can move a long way in the right direction in the meantime.

Key Steps on the Journey

There are four important things that have to happen for the process of purification to be effective and for the journey to lead toward sexual wholeness. Sometimes we may discuss just one of these components with our children and other times we may weave all four together in order to discuss a particular topic that has come up. Our goal is to make sure that we are including each of these components in our discussions with our children on a fairly regular basis.

The four components to mentoring a child toward sexual wholeness are:

- Know What You're Aiming For
- Tell Your Story
- Developing Emotional Resilience
- Have Regular Cleansing Conversations

Know What You're Aiming For

We have to hold up something for our children to aim for. I do not mean that we are to hold ourselves up as perfect examples for them to emulate. I am talking about teaching our children God's design and purpose for sex.

In case you are wondering, I am not about to give you a Sunday School lesson. Many parents do not really know what God's design for sex is. Many pastors do not know what God's design for sex is either. God's design for sex is not typically on the curriculum in theological training. I am not trying to blame anyone, but we should not continue in ignorance.

This is where my background comes in handy. My education is in the field of biology and teaching biology. I will try not to geek out on you too much. From an adult point of view there are actually many fascinating aspects of sexuality we can examine from a biological and even theological point of view. There is a lot more to human sexuality than most people are aware of. There is no need to go into all of that with a child, however. To keep it simple, here are five key points our children eventually need to know about the purpose of sex.

1: Sex Is God's Idea

We cannot escape the reality that God created sex on purpose. It was his idea. Furthermore, God did not create Adam and Eve and tell them to keep their clothes on. He told them to multiply. God actually encouraged them to have sex.

> *God blessed them; and God said to them,*
> *"Be fruitful and multiply, and fill the earth..."*[5]
> *—The Prophet Moses*

> *And God blessed Noah and his sons and said to them,*
> *"Be fruitful and multiply, and fill the earth."*[6]
> *—The Prophet Moses*

---

[5] Genesis 1:28 (NASB)

[6] Genesis 9:1 (NASB)

Sex is God's idea. Plants and many animals reproduce in ways that do not require contact. He could have made us reproduce without contact too, but He did not. He intended for sex to be exactly what it is. We do not need to be embarrassed to talk about what God was not embarrassed to create.

2: Sex Bonds a Husband and Wife

The act of sex bonds the people together who participated. I do not mean theoretically, but quite literally. This bonding is essentially permanent and is so on purpose. Morality aside, it is wise to restrict sexual union to the person we plan on staying with permanently: our spouse. It is good to explain to children, when they are old enough to understand, that this bonding is quite real.

In humans, sexual intercourse causes the hormone oxytocin to be released, causing an emotional bond to form between the two people engaging in sex.[7] The brains of each person actually change so that the next time they see each other they will feel an emotional attraction to the other. Each time they have sex this bond is strengthened.

God created this process. Therefore, we can comfortably conclude that God intends for sex to be something that bonds a husband and wife emotionally. In other words, sex helps keep a husband and wife together. The Bible refers to a couple feeling like one flesh when they are joined through sex. This is not a spiritual euphemism; something is really happening to make us feel that way.

> *For this reason a man shall leave his father and his mother,*
> *and be joined to his wife; and they shall become one flesh.*[8]
> *—The Prophet Moses*

Scientists understand that repeated sexual intercourse increases this emotional bond between couples. Perhaps this is part of the reason Paul advised husbands and wives to not refrain from sexual intimacy:

---

[7] Neumann, Inga D. "Oxytocin: The Neuropeptide of Love Reveals Some of It's Secrets," *Cell Metabolism,* 5.4 (2007): 231-233

[8] Genesis 2:24 (NASB)

The wife does not have authority over her own body, but the husband does; and likewise also the husband does not have authority over his own body, but the wife does. Stop depriving one another, except by agreement for a time, so that you may devote yourselves to prayer, and come together again so that Satan will not tempt you because of your lack of self-control. But this I say by way of concession, not of command.[9]
—The Apostle Paul

We can admit that there are marriages where sex can leave one or both partners feeling something other than bonded. We do not want this for our children, but this is a form of sexual brokenness that can happen. However, when sex is used as God designed, it enhances marital bonding and reduces temptation as well.

3: Sex is Intended to be Enjoyed

If we look further in Scripture, we see that God was not just interested in Adam and Eve creating children. King Solomon encourages his sons to enjoy sex as God designed:

Let your fountain be blessed,
And rejoice in the wife of your youth.[10]
—King Solomon

The Song of Solomon expresses a purpose of sex other than reproduction as well:

You have made my heart beat faster, my sister, my bride; you have made my heart beat faster with a single glance of your eyes[11]
—The Groom

May my beloved come into his garden and eat its choice fruits![12]
—The Bride

---

[9] 1 Corinthians 7:4–6 (NASB)

[10] Proverbs 5:18 (NASB)

[11] Song of Solomon 4:9 (NASB)

[12] Song of Solomon 4:16b (NASB)

God made sex to be extremely pleasurable—and He does not do anything by accident. Sex is for us to enjoy within marriage.

Again we should pause and acknowledge that one of the forms sexual brokenness can take is to wound us in such a way that we do not enjoy sex. This was never God's intention but a result of brokenness. If this is true of a parent we can still tell a child what God's design is intended to be. Our children do not have to experience the same sexual brokenness we did.

4: Sex is Intended to be Selfless

We are all aware of situations where sex between spouses is misused and drives one partner away. This can happen when one or both parties approach sex as something to take rather than to give. Sex is perhaps the most vulnerable act we ever partake in, and as such, can easily feel unsafe if one spouse is taking more than giving.

This is perfectly in line with biblical teaching about love in general. We do not take love; we give it for the benefit of others.

> *Love is patient, love is kind. It does not envy, it does not*
> *boast, it is not proud. It does not dishonor others, it is not*
> *self-seeking, it is not easily angered,*
> *it keeps no record of wrongs.*[13]
> *—The Apostle Paul*

The worldly view of sex is that of taking. The godly view of sex is that of giving ourselves, as Christ gave Himself for us. Christ gave Himself for us, in spite of all we did against Him. Likewise the husband and wife are to give to each other, in spite of each other's imperfections. As the wedding vow goes, "in sickness and health, for richer or poorer, for better or worse, until death." This is how Christ gave to us, and how we are to give to each other. Our children need to know that sex is meant to be an act of giving, not taking.

5: Sex is Spiritual

Throughout scripture a comparison is made between marital sex and our union with God or Jesus. This may sound strange to our

---

[13] 1 Corinthians 13:4–5 (NIV) emphasis added

ears, but people in biblical times were apparently more comfortable with such ideas.

> For He says, "The two shall become one flesh." But the one
> who joins himself to the Lord is one spirit with Him.[14]
> —The Apostle Paul

> For I am jealous for you with a godly jealousy;
> for I betrothed you to one husband, so that to Christ
> I might present you as a pure virgin.[15]
> —The Apostle Paul

In the Bible, sexual intercourse in marriage is directly compared to our union with Christ. There are many other scriptures from Isaiah to Revelation that repeat this analogy.

Understanding this biblical view of sex is helpful to parents, so that we understand that part of the holy purpose of sex is to give us a taste of what meeting Christ will be like. Sex has a holy purpose of bonding a husband and wife, as well as giving us a sense of anticipation to meet Christ in heaven. This is why sexuality is sacred.

Tell Your Story

Telling our story is part of the parenting process. It is part of what "Honest Talk" means. It is also particularly helpful in starting conversations about sex with older children.

Young children will enter into almost any conversation we start with them. They are not particularly good at considering what other people are thinking or feeling and have a hard time imagining their parents were ever children. Sharing our story with young children is usually in the form of what happened last week or some time period that they can remember.

Older children, roughly around age ten and up, can think abstractly. They can imagine their parents being young. They are becoming aware that other people have their own feelings and

---

14 1 Corinthians 6:16–17 (NASB)

15 2 Corinthians 11:2 (NASB)

experiences. They are also slightly less willing to enter into personal conversations, especially if they are a little embarrassed about something. This is where our story really becomes powerful.

With older children, and especially with teenagers, the very best way to broach a sensitive topic is to first convey the understanding that we know very well what the child is feeling inside. We do this by telling part of our story that is:

- Something that happened when we were their age
- Something similar to what we are talking about

Sometimes the age we experienced something is different than the age our child experienced a similar event. We don't have to be specific. We can say, "When I was around your age," or "When I was a kid." The goal is to create a connection point of shared experience.

An Example of Using Story

Let us say that we discovered our child purposefully found a way to access pornography. We know they are embarrassed and feel guilty and probably don't want to talk to us about what happened. Even before we ask them for details of what happened we might consider sharing our story. A parent with this experience could share with the child a time they purposefully viewed pornography, trying to select a time as close as possible to our child's age.

We don't need to go into a lot of detail, but just enough that they understand we know what they probably feel like. We can share why we looked at pornography, how we felt when we were viewing it, and how we felt later when reflecting on what we had done. All the while the child's anxiety is lowering and they are feeling understood by one of the most important people in their life. Sharing our story becomes perhaps the most affirming thing we can do for our child, even before they share what they did.

Throughout this book we will review how we might share our story as it relates to each topic we discuss. Story is that important.

Considerations When Telling Your Story

Let's review and expand upon safety precautions we should take when sharing our story with our children. When sharing some portion of our own sexual past with our children, we should:

1. **Share broad categories, not details**. For example, you can explain that you have been exposed to pornography or say you saw "naked pictures of people" without describing in detail what you saw.

2. **Have already shared the same information with our spouse**. It is completely inappropriate to burden a child with sexual secrets. If we cannot be or have not been honest with our spouse about something in our sexual past or present, it is not okay to share that with our child. Don't let this shut you down. Instead, make this an opportunity to grow closer to your spouse. Perhaps it is time to get away with your spouse and share more of your past with each other. Our spouse is not someone to hide past shame from, but someone to help heal those scars.

3. **Have already begun steps to address any lingering unwanted sexual behaviors.** Our children need to see an example of how to address sexual brokenness. We do not need to be completely free of unwanted behaviors, but we do need to have taken steps to address them before sharing those with our child. It is one thing to say, "I looked at pornography when I was your age," or even "I still have to work on avoiding pornography, but I have friends who help me." It is quite another to tell a child about past pornography use if the parent is still looking at pornography, has no plan on how to stop, has never tried to learn how to stop, and has not told their spouse.

4. **Never treat a child as an accountability partner.** There is an element of two-way sharing in accountability with an older child, which we will discuss a bit later. This is how we teach what Biblical, mutual accountability is. However, a child should not be put in the role of a parent's primary support for the parent's sexual integrity. This puts an inappropriate burden on the child.

5. **Consider the child's personality.** Each child is unique and will respond differently to hearing their parent has engaged in unhealthy behavior. When you do tell some of your story, watch your child's face carefully. If you see them

looking panicked or frightened, stop and ask how they are feeling. If you sense what you are telling them is too much for them, then stop sharing and assure and comfort them.

The purpose of telling our story is to help them realize that we understand what sexual temptation feels like. We are creating a deeper bond to make discussions about sexuality more effective in the future. It must be a goal in our story telling to do no harm.

Developing Emotional Resilience

Emotions are tightly intertwined with our sexuality. As such, it is ineffective to try to guide our children toward sexual purity without teaching them to understand and effectively resolve their emotions. Without resilience or strength in handling emotions a child will be unable to make progress in their sexual wholeness. Parenting for sexual wholeness requires us to talk at least as often with our children about their emotions as we talk about sex.

There are two primary reasons we need to talk frequently with our children about emotions. The first is that it prepares them to have conversations about sex. The second is that it helps them avoid sexual temptation when they are teenagers.

Talking about Emotions Prepares for Talking about Sex

Sexuality is very personal. If we wait until our children are teenagers to talk about anything personal and then want them to talk with us about sex, we will likely find they are unwilling to do so. The solution to this dilemma is to demonstrate to our children when they are young that our family talks about personal things and that this is a good thing.

Emotions are personal. Talking about emotions feels personal and intimate. When we talk with our young children about their feelings on a regular basis, they become comfortable discussing personal things. When we do this, it is not so great a stretch to begin talking about sexual feelings when they are twelve or thirteen. Talking about emotions is the training ground for later discussions about sexuality.

Emotional Resilience Reduces Sexual Temptation

Uncomfortable emotions can play into lust when not addressed effectively. Unpleasant emotions can cause our children to want to escape. Sexual fantasy, pornography, and masturbation are particularly good at masking negative feelings, and can become a child's default go-to as a way of escape. Teaching emotional awareness will help them find other ways to deal with painful emotions.

Resolving unpleasant emotions occurs through relationships with each other and with God. The earlier we start training our children do deal with emotions, the more effective our teaching will be. Emotional awareness prepares children to react maturely to disappointment and stress rather than escape into fantasy.

Much of an older child or teenagers draw to fantasy and pornography is not so much about a sex drive but a deep desire to escape emotional pain. We will look more closely at the process behind this later in the book. For now we just want to understand that our older children and teenagers need to know what to do with unpleasant feelings they experience. This greatly reduces the number of times they feel tempted to escape into some form of lust.

Have Regular Cleansing Conversations

None of us would give a six-year-old a bath and then consider the job of physical cleansing forever finished. No parent would tell a ten-year-old to take a shower and expect them to stay clean until they leave home at age eighteen. We all know better than to give a twelve-year-old a toothbrush and expect them to keep their teeth clean without another reminder to brush. Yet for the last few generations this has been the typical parenting approach to sexual integrity.

Kids get dirty. Sometimes they jump in the mud on purpose; other times it gets on them as they simply walk around. It doesn't really matter if it's their fault or not. One bath or one toothbrushing is not enough. Children need regular cleansing. Sexuality is no different, especially in this century.

No matter how much we try to protect our children, they simply will be exposed to pornography and sexual misinformation in the world they are growing up in. While we should always strive to protect them from contamination, we must realize that our primary focus should be on "cleaning them up" through our relationship and conversations with them. Because the world is going to "throw dirt at them" on a regular basis, our open communication with them must also occur on a regular basis.

Our children get "cleaned up" from sexual misinformation through discussion with God and us. We will call these "cleansing conversations." Like a bath or brushing teeth, these conversations need to happen on a frequent basis. The longer we go between conversations, the more the dirt will build up on our children in between.

Cleansing conversations are a form of instruction in that they instruct our children how to deal with their emotions and sexuality. The best training and instruction occurs through the process of asking questions and sharing thoughts, which are what cleansing conversations are. We will discuss how to have these conversations throughout the rest of this book.

Different, not More Work

I want to be careful not to lose any parents at this point. Some readers may be feeling a new burden has just been placed on them. This is not supposed to feel like "more work" a parent has to do. It is instead "different" work. You are already in relationship and communication with your kids. All you have to do is change the subject of your conversations from time to time.

Some parents will have very frequent conversations about sexuality with their children. Others will do so not nearly as often, but more than they are doing now. There is no specific frequency these conversations need to happen. Every child is different and their needs for cleansing conversations are different. Every parent is different and their ability to have these conversations is not the same. Find what works for you and your child and do that. This is not a contest. Whatever you and your child are able to do will help.

The rest of this book will walk you through specific cleansing conversations and emotional resilience activities you can do with your children at appropriate ages. There will be times we point you to other resources when a topic has already been very well covered by other authors.

Parent Challenge

Share with your spouse or another parent the following:

1. How did you think God viewed sex when you were a teenager?

2. What can you keep in mind that will help you react well when your child demonstrates sexual brokenness?

3. Did your parents encourage you to express emotions or were there emotions that your parents tried to stop you from expressing or talking about?

PART TWO
Working with Our Children

4

Introducing Emotions to Young Children

We will now look at activities and conversations to have with younger children up to age eight. If your child is older than eight, you might want to skim through this chapter to see if any ideas mentioned still might be helpful for your older child. No matter what age your child is, you will want to be sure they understand these concepts eventually.

We Share Our Emotions

The first thing to teach a child about emotions and feelings is that we are to share them with each other. We do not writhe on the floor and cry; we explain how we feel to someone near us. If we do not learn to share the burden of our feelings with others, we become vulnerable to depression. King Solomon wrote:

A joyful heart makes a cheerful face, but when the heart is sad, the spirit is broken.[16]

---

[16] Proverbs 15:13 (NASB)

Learning how to cope with difficult emotions is critical for any of us to thrive, including our children. We find wisdom again from Solomon:

Two are better than one because they have a good return for their labor. For if either of them falls, the one will lift up his companion. But woe to the one who falls when there is not another to lift him up. Furthermore, if two lie down together they keep warm, but how can one be warm alone? And if one can overpower him who is alone, two can resist him. A cord of three strands is not quickly torn apart.[17]

We are advised to not live life alone, but in community with each other. We were not meant to endure life, including stress and difficult emotions, alone. The apostle Paul expounds on King Solomon's words:

Bear one another's burdens, and thereby fulfill the law of Christ.[18]

Our Father never intended for any of us, including our children, to endure emotional pain in isolation. We are instructed to help each other through our feelings, so that we do not give in to destructive behavior as a way of escape. Notice that Paul did not say to *solve* each other's problems, as that is not always possible. He is simply talking about being with each other through hard times.

We want our children to become accustomed to bringing their burdens to others. The younger we can instill this pattern in them, the better. When our children are very young, simply inviting them to "tell us about it" is often enough when they are feeling down. We eventually want to teach our children that they can also bring their feelings to God.

Blessed be the Lord, who daily bears our burden, the God who is our salvation.[19]
—King David

---

[17] Ecclesiastes 4:9–12 (NASB)
[18] Galatians 6:2 (NASB)
[19] Psalm 68:19 (NASB)

Our children are born trusting us, but they are not born with any knowledge of Christ. We model Christ to them, particularly when they are young. We must first model to them the compassion of Christ by offering comfort to them when they experience negative feelings. Our children must experience being comforted by us, who they can see, before we can expect them to bring their emotional burdens before God, who they cannot see. As our children mature, we guide them to finding the same kind of comfort in the arms of God.

Expanding Emotional Vocabulary

Before our children can experience the comfort of being heard and understood, they must be able to express what they are feeling. In their younger years, this means helping them expand their vocabulary beyond the simple feelings of mad, sad, and happy. Those simple words do not tell us much about what is going on inside our children. We want to help them share more of what they are experiencing inside. This will help them feel more fully understood by others.

Expand Emotional Vocabulary with Story

We can enlarge our child's emotional vocabulary through children's stories. It is very common for children's books to talk about the feelings of a character. There are even book series for children specifically designed to teach feelings. Books with pictures are particularly helpful for younger children, as they often show expressions clearly on a character's face. See Appendix B for a list of books you could use to point out feelings.

As we read to our child, we can slow down when a book talks about a feeling or shows an expression, and then ask our child what that character is feeling. We can ask if they have ever felt that way. We could share about a time when we felt that way. Then we can continue with the story.

From time to time, when you are reading stories that demonstrate feelings, you can tell your child that God made our feelings. Sometimes these make us feel good, and other times they make us feel bad. You can point out that feelings that make us feel bad help us know it is time to talk to someone else about what we are feeling.

Teach That Emotions Are Safe

During a story when a character is described as having emotions, ask the child if it is okay to feel that way. For example, if a character is said to be lonely, we could ask, "Do you think it's okay to feel lonely sometimes?" Don't argue if you think their answer is not quite right; instead, say something like, "Well, I think it's okay to feel lonely. Everyone feels lonely sometimes. We don't stay lonely forever, just for a while." The point of such discussion is to help a child see that we don't have to fear negative emotions, because they are not permanent.

To reinforce this, parents should not overreact to a child expressing emotions. Parents who behave anxiously when a child is upset only pass that anxiety on to their children. We should strive to remain calm even if our child is very distraught. Our calm teaches children that even bad feelings are okay. This may take practice, but it is worth the effort to portray a calm sense of security during what may feel to our children like an emotional trauma.

Expand Emotional Vocabulary with a Feelings Chart

A feelings chart is a sheet full of faces, each showing a different expression. There are typically names for each feeling below each facial expression. We have included one for boys and one for girls in Appendix A of this book.

A feelings chart can be used for straightforward teaching. We can show the chart to a child and explain, "God made all of these emotions, and all of them help us know what we need to do." The idea we hope our children slowly understand is that, while some emotions feel bad, they are still helpful to us as they point us toward getting the help we need. We can use the chart in a number of ways to help children learn to identify what they are feeling.

Ann Martin, a licensed clinical social worker who does a lot of work with children, shared the following story of how the use of a the feelings chart paid off with her own girls:

I remember when my girls were three and five and we were all in my youngest girl's room putting up new curtains. I could tell that my five-year-old was starting to feel something and with her that usually came out as anger. I just watched her and then pretty soon she said, 'Mom, come here I wanna show you something.' I went into her room and she pulled out her feelings chart and she pointed to jealously and she said, 'That's how I'm feeling.'

I said, 'I'm so glad you talked about it.' Then we talked through it, explaining not everyone gets the same things all the time. We assured her we loved her the same as her sister, and she felt better. All she needed was to tell me how she felt. She wanted me to hear it. I didn't try to make her feel better or say we would buy her something too, I just let her talk about it and she was better.[20]

Using a feelings chart is especially helpful for younger children, because they don't even have to be able to read for it to help them identify feelings. On the other hand feelings charts are used even with adults in counseling, so don't think you need to limit its use to only very young children.

Model How Feelings Are Shared

We should model for our children how to share feelings. Much of what younger children learn comes from watching their parents, and this includes how to express feelings.

A parent could make a point to share emotions that came up during their day with the family. It is important that we share as many positive feelings as negative with our children. We want our children to be aware of times they feel proud, hopeful, and valued. This helps them develop a sense of gratitude, which is becoming rare in children today.

For example, a parent might say, "My boss told me she really appreciates my work today. That made me feel valued." I realize that the word "valued" is not on the sample feelings chart provided at the

---

[20] Ann Martin, LCSW, *Pure Parenting Seminar,* Beaverton, OR (2015)

end of this book, but we can expand our child's vocabulary beyond the few feelings on that chart.

A young child might not know what "valued" means. With a very young child you might say "happy," but I do encourage you to expand your child's emotional vocabulary as soon as you can. A five year old can learn to understand what it means to feel valued.

Conversations like this demonstrate that sharing feelings is just part of what we do, not something restricted to times we teach.

Of course, we need to express our painful emotions in front of our children as well. We might say, "I felt embarrassed because I tried really hard on a new recipe today, and it ended up tasting really bad."

You may notice it is hard to come up with words to express feelings when you avoid, "mad, sad, and happy." That is because few adults have much training in emotional awareness. Don't let that stop you. Get the feelings chart out and refer to it yourself to find a more specific word to use. It is okay if it takes you some time to get good at this. You and your child can learn together.

Don't Fix Feelings

We don't "fix" feelings. If a child is looking sad, we do not say, "Aw, don't be sad." This approach teaches a child that it is bad to feel sad. It's not bad to feel sad. There are some very appropriate times to feel sad. Instead, ask them questions to help them determine what is behind their sadness. Talking through that is more helpful than trying to shut down their feelings.

The message we want to teach our children is, "In this house, it is okay to have feelings and to talk about them." Many of us grew up in homes where there was an unwritten rule to not discuss certain feelings. We don't want to put our kids in that emotional straight jacket.

Likewise, if a child attempts to soothe us when we display a negative emotion, we can help them see that, while soothing is good, the point is not to drive emotions away. For example, if you are feeling overwhelmed because you have so much to do and your child comes with an anxious expression and says, "Don't feel sad," you can smile at him or her and say, "I feel a little overwhelmed by all the things I need to do this weekend, but I'm also okay. Everyone feels overwhelmed sometimes."

Model Bringing Emotions to God

Our children do not automatically know to bring their feelings to God. We must model this for them. We hope you pray with your children. When you do, let them hear you bringing your emotions to Him for help. Let them hear you say things like, "Father, I feel embarrassed at how I acted today. Help me remember that you love me anyway." A prayer like this teaches not only that we can bring our feelings to God, but also that He loves us in spite of what our feelings or actions have been. This is a critical reality for our children to understand.

Messing Up Emotionally

It is only fair to recognize that dealing with emotions is an area where we parents mess up rather frequently. Our lives are not as neat as the storybooks we read to our kids, but this too is okay.

God knows we are incapable of perfection. That's why He sent Jesus to intervene on our behalf. We are made holy not by our actions but through Jesus's sacrifice. We must keep this in mind throughout our imperfect attempts at parenting.

We can't demonstrate perfection to our kids. They couldn't live up to that even if we could—and again, we can't. We will have to apologize to them, possibly often, for not reacting well to our own emotions. They are not going to react well to their emotions all the time either, so our imperfection will actually make them feel more normal, not less.

When Parents Mess Up

Our children need to see what a person should do after reacting badly. Remember, our failures are what qualify us to mentor our children.

How do we handle it when we realize that the reaction we just gave was over the top or even hurtful? Do we apologize to our family? Do we say we need a little time to calm down and step away for a while? Do we accept our family's love for us afterward? What we do after reacting poorly to our own emotions is a lesson just as important as anything else we teach about emotions.

Mentoring our children with their emotions will point out flaws in our own personalities, and that is a good thing. As we become more emotionally aware ourselves, we will slowly become better parents to our children and better people for everyone else to be around as well. For most of us, handling emotions well will be a journey we take *with* our kids, not something we have mastered to pass on to them.

Preparing for the Future

At this point, you may be wondering again why we are talking so much about emotions when this book is for teaching children about sex. You may even be wondering if you bought the right book!

The reason we talk so much about emotions is because understanding what we are feeling, being able to talk about that clearly with others, and learning to react appropriately to feelings are foundational to sexual wholeness.

As we have said, talking about something as personal as feelings at age five prepares a child to talk about even more personal topics about sexuality when they are twelve. Frequently discussing feelings when young makes a child more comfortable discussing sex when they are older.

We also mentioned that an inability to deal with negative emotions is a primary cause for sexual brokenness later on. This happens when a child uses some form of sexual stimulation as a means of escaping unpleasant feelings. Teaching a child to handle disappointment and uncomfortable feelings now reduces their perceived need to escape into fantasy, pornography, and masturbation when they are adolescents.

Sexual urges are also feelings. They are very powerful feelings. We must first teach our children to manage simpler feelings, long before sexual urges hit them like a semi-truck. If they have not learned to react appropriately to the feeling of being left out by their friends, how will they possibly be able to deal with the urge to view pornography once their hormones kick in? Emotional awareness training for a five-year-old prepares him or her for dealing with the much stronger feelings that will come when they are twelve or thirteen.

Emotional awareness at a young age is a critical foundation that honest talk about sex is built on.

Parent-Child Activity: Option 1

I Had That Feeling Once

Tell your children you are reading this book, and that it gave you an assignment you would like their help with. You can do this with any child age four and up.

Instructions:

1. Turn to the feelings charts in Appendix A and show them to your children.
2. Tell them your assignment is to pick a feeling and ask everyone in the family to share a time they felt that way.
3. Let one of the children pick a feeling
4. You go first, sharing a time when you felt that way and how you reacted.
5. Let each other members of the family do the same.

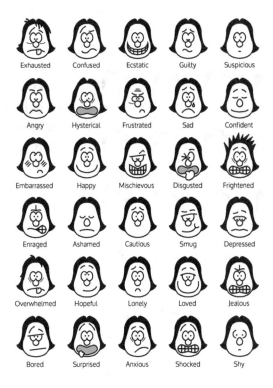

39

Parent-Child Activity: Option 2

Name That Feeling

Tell your children you are reading this book, and that it gave you an assignment you would like their help with. You can do this with any child age four and up.

Instructions:

1. Go to http://downloads.purelifeacademy.org and download either the boy or girl faces chart. These are the ones with no names of feelings.
2. Print the chart.
3. Cut up the chart so that each face is a separate piece of paper. We will call each piece of paper a card.
4. Put all the "cards" in a hat, basket, or bowl.
5. Have a child draw a card, and then try to name the feeling the face is showing.
6. Have the person who drew the card tell a time when they felt that way.
7. Move on to the next person.

NOTE: You can start with only the easier emotions for younger children. You will know best which emotions your children will be familiar with.

It doesn't matter if the emotion a child names is exactly correct, as long as it makes sense compared to the face on the card.

5

Cleansing Conversations
for Young Children

Begin Early

There is an element of truth to the saying, "use it or lose it," when it comes to taking advantage of the openness young children have to a parent's help. Young children have an eagerness to be dependent on others—which is a quality that does not last long. I believe it is this quality that Jesus was referring to when He spoke to his disciples about children.

> *At that time the disciples came to Jesus and asked,*
> *"Who, then, is the greatest in the kingdom of heaven?"*
> *He called a little child to Him, and placed the child among*
> *them. And He said: "Truly I tell you, unless you change and*
> *become like little children, you will never enter the kingdom*
> *of heaven."*[21]
> *—Jesus*

The younger a child is, the more he willingly relies on his parents. A child of two typically has no interest in tying her own

---

[21] Matthew 18:1–3 (NIV)

shoes, but at eight may protest aggressively if someone tries to tie her shoes for her. Children are happily reliant on adults when they are young. God wants us to rely on Him without question, just as a young child does his parents.

But we all know this happy dependence does not last. Our children will want to do things without help more and more as they grow. We need to capitalize on our children's openness to outside help while they are still young.

Create Openness—before the Need Arises

When it comes to sexual integrity, our children will need us most in their teenage years. We've all been teenagers, however, and know that the teen years are a time when children are the least interested in getting help from their parents. If we wait until the teen years to begin guiding them toward sexual wholeness, the chances that they will cooperate are slim. We should begin when they are at an age when they are most open to our counsel and are most honest with us. We set the pattern at a young age, so that talking about sexuality becomes normal before children reach an age where it is harder for them to confide in their parents.

The following sections outline conversations with younger children that serve to clean away any sexual misinformation they encounter that may otherwise pollute their view of sex.

Answer Questions

When our children are young, teaching sexuality is primarily in the form of answering a child's questions. A child often lets the parent know that it is time to give new information about sexuality by asking questions. Even if we feel startled by the questions of our young children, we can be assured that if they ask the question, they are ready to know the answer.

However, when a child does ask a question, this does not mean we need to overwhelm them with everything we know. For example, if a five-year-old asks, "Where do babies come from?" we may find that all we need to say is, "Babies come from mommies." Often that is all the child wants to know. If they ask more, we could add,

"Babies come from mommies' tummies." A child of five does not need to be aware of sex. We answer honestly, not trying to withhold information, but not giving them more than they want to know.

It is possible of course that a child is particularly curious and keeps asking "why" or "how," until the parent must either lie or give an answer that feels like too much to tell a young child. In that case, we should still answer, but be as non-graphic as possible. Again, if a child really wants to know, it is best to tell her. Otherwise she is going to ask a peer, an older child, or the computer, and the information she gains from these sources is often a twisted version of the truth and never what a parent wants their child to hear or see. The guideline is simple: *If they want to know, they are old enough to know.*

On the other hand, children may be very shy in asking questions they have about sexuality. If a child asks no questions about sex by age eight, that may mean they have none. In our current culture, however, it is extremely likely that a child will be exposed to some form of sexual misinformation before age eight. This is why it is usually best to be proactive and give your child at least some information.

When it is time to provide age-appropriate information about sex to younger children, which includes the differences between male and female bodies, for example, it is helpful to use books written by experts. Many excellent Christian resources already exist to help you with this, some of which are listed in Appendix B of this book.

Remember That Sex Is Good

An overarching theme in all our discussions about sex and sexuality with our children must be that it was designed to be a wonderful thing. If all we ever discuss is how sex can go wrong, our children can become crippled in their own ability to achieve intimacy with their future spouses. It is biblical and accurate to portray the general topic of sex as something to be celebrated rather than shunned.

We want to portray to our children that they are seeking information about something that is good. We can be careful of our facial expressions and word choices when our children ask us questions about sex. We can begin our replies with "I'm glad you asked," when they ask a question about sex. We can be careful how we act and talk when referring to sexual organs, to show respect rather than disgust. We never want to shame our children about their own bodies or project shame toward others' bodies.

Once we start talking to our children, we need to be prepared for them to tell us that they have already been exposed to sexual information. We need to be ready to discuss what the child has been exposed to and answer any questions with the truth, correcting any misinformation they have picked up.

Personal Boundaries

Personal boundaries related to sexuality are something that our society talks about a lot. It is important to explain to children that their body belongs to them and that other people may not touch any place covered with undergarments without permission. This is a fairly basic concept but if you want more help addressing it with your child, see Appendix B where we list recommended resources on personal safety.

It is also important to teach them the concepts of privacy and modesty. The point of modesty is not to hide something shameful about ourselves but something special and private.

> *On the contrary, those parts of the body that seem to be weaker are indispensable, and the parts that we think are less honorable we treat with special honor. And **the parts that are unpresentable are treated with special modesty**, while our presentable parts need no special treatment.*[22]
> *—The Apostle Paul*

Paul uses body parts as an example how to treat spiritual gifts of believers. He compares our body parts with spiritual gifts, and in

---

[22] 1 Corinthians 12:22–24 (NIV) emphasis added

doing so says our private parts have "abundant honor" or "special honor." According to scripture our sexual organs are not dishonorable, but are especially honorable, thus deserving special treatment and modesty. This biblical viewpoint can help explain to our children why modesty is important.

There is a balance to be had here. On the one hand, we want to teach our children modesty between those of opposite genders after a certain age. On the other hand, we do not want a child to be ashamed of his own body. This said if a parent accidentally sees an older child of either gender naked, or an older child sees a parent, the parent should not act alarmed or offended. To do so could cause a child to believe there is something wrong with her. It is okay to be embarrassed—it's even okay to laugh (with the child, not at him or her). Our sexual organs may be treated with honor and thus concealed, but they are good and not to be ashamed of if accidentally exposed.

I asked my friend and social worker Ann Martin to give us some pointers on boundaries and young children.

I am a huge advocate of teaching personal boundaries. I worked with a lot of abused kids before I had kids, so I taught my daughters, "Your body's yours; no one else gets to see it or to touch it unless you give them permission." When they were little there was a time when their dad would give them a bath; but there was a time when we stopped that and only I gave them baths. I wanted them to be comfortable with the fact that males don't need to see them naked.

We also have an open-door policy where the bedroom doors stay open when someone is over, and even if my two daughters are together in the same room. The door has to stay open, and I can walk by and check in. I just know too many stories of how allowing children to play behind closed doors can go wrong. When a friend would come over and the friend would shut the door, I would go in and open the

door and say, "Remember we're leaving the door open,"
and they were fine with that.²³

Know Where Your Children Are

Protect your children by knowing whom they are with and where they are. It's okay to have a rule that you must get to know the parents of a family before allowing your young child to play in their house. It's okay to ask another parent if they allow their children to play behind closed doors. It's okay not to allow your child to spend time with kids you have a bad feeling about, even if you aren't certain why. It is okay to tell your child, "I just don't know them very well, so I'd rather you bring them to our house than you going to theirs."

Set an example and tell your children who you are with and what you do when you are away from the house. Make it a normal way of life for family members to share this information.

Finally, ask your kids what they are doing when they are away. Don't interrogate them—be interested in them. This will help you determine where and with whom your child is safe. You should share what you do when you are away as an example.

Provide Affection

We cannot talk about cleansing through relationship without discussing the physical aspect of relationships. Unfortunately, our American culture has increasingly equated any physical contact with sexuality. That was never God's intent. Physical affection was never meant to be restricted to sexual expression. Examples in scripture point out that followers of God have, since the beginning, welcomed physical affection:

So when Laban heard the news of Jacob his sister's son,
he ran to meet him, and embraced him and kissed him
and brought him to his house²⁴.
—The Prophet Moses

---

²³ Ibid
²⁴ Genesis 29:13a (NASB)

*Then Esau ran to meet him [Jacob] and embraced him,
and fell on his neck and kissed him, and they wept.*[25]
—The Prophet Moses

*So he [the Prodigal Son] got up and came to his father. But
while he was still a long way off, his father saw him and felt
compassion for him, and ran and embraced him and kissed
him.*[26]
—The Apostle Luke

*And they [the elders at the church of Ephesus] began to
weep aloud and embraced Paul, and repeatedly kissed
him.*[27]
—The Apostle Luke

It is worth noting that, while certainly women embraced each
other in biblical times, these are all examples of men hugging and
kissing other men—in the Bible, of all things! Our fathers of faith
embraced physical affection and so should we.

Our children are wired by God Himself to need physical touch.
Children are not likely to receive positive physical touch outside the
home in this day and age, however. Where I live, teachers are no
longer allowed to touch a child at all because school districts fear
being accused of some form of abuse. Whether or not this is a wise
choice is not the point. The reality is, as our culture changes, your
child is less and less likely to experience positive touch unless it
happens at home.

Children need to be hugged and held by both parents, not just
Mom. This is extremely important and helps them develop a sense
of security and being loved. To ignore this need is to leave a child in
need of intimacy and more vulnerable to seeking intimacy through
pornography or sexual behavior. My personal story reflects this truth.

I had a very stable home life. My parents talked about God a lot
and provided excellent examples for me to follow. My mother did

---

[25] Genesis 33:4 (NASB)
[26] Luke 15:20 (NASB)
[27] Acts 20:37 (NASB)

hug and hold me, especially up through age nine or so. My father, on the other hand, had grown up in a very dysfunctional family and did not know how to show affection. I have no memory of him ever hugging me. That left me feeling both an intense need for affection from role models but also afraid of affection. This became a large contributing factor to the problems with sexual behavior and pornography use I developed as a young person.

I grew up feeling very awkward hugging or receiving hugs from anyone. As a child, I could not imagine God wanting to hug me, which was harmful to my image of him. Since I had no physical intimacy, I sought out intimacy through pornography, fantasy, and sex. It was quite difficult as an adult to unlearn my misconception that physical affection could only come through sex or that it was innately sexual in nature. I did not want that for my children, so I was sure to give each of them lots of hugs and to hold them often. We save our children a lot of grief when we give them the affection they need, so they don't need to seek it out elsewhere.

Discuss the Reality of Pornography

Some parents fear that bringing up the topic of pornography with a younger child may make them curious and want to seek it out. While it's easy to see how such a concern would arise, every expert I've asked advises that it is better to warn a child about pornography than to remain silent. Pornography is a very broken form of sexuality and its modern day form is extremely harmful to children. The question parents should ask themselves is, do I want my child to learn about pornography by being exposed to it, or by me explaining to them what it is? Remember, it is no longer a question of *if* a child will be exposed to pornography, but *when*.

How do young children get exposed to pornography? One cause is accidental discovery when using an Internet device while unsupervised. But even if we completely restrict Internet access at home, we cannot stop exposure.

One parent told me that his eight-year-old was shown pornography while at a same-aged friend's house, and that friend was from their church. Another friend of mine told me that her six-year-old was shown pornography on a school bus, through another child's cell phone.

I wish it were true that children younger than nine were too young to know what pornography is. In the distant past that may have been true, but it is not any longer. We need to prepare our children for what they will face.

When to Address Pornography

Here are some basic guidelines for knowing when it is time to explain what pornography is:

- Warn your children about the possibility of being shown pornography somewhere between ages six and eight, depending on how much exposure they have to other kids and the Internet. Appendix B lists resources to help you talk to children of different ages.
- If your child tells you they saw pictures of naked people, the cat is out of the bag—it's time to talk about it.
- Talk to your child if you catch or discover his or her pornography use.
- If you overhear a conversation between your child and their friend turn sexual, even just a little, talk to him. This indicates that he is becoming aware of sexuality, meaning it's time to start talking.
- If you are with your child and she takes notice when a nude or partially nude image appears, talk to her. This could happen in a mall, while watching TV, or almost anywhere these days. If we see our children notice and stare, it's time to talk.

What Not to Do

Don't refer to pornography as "disgusting," or some other shameful term. A child may take a while to understand the difference between the beauty God created the human body to have versus pornography, which depicts sex as degrading and self-centered. We can accidentally send the message that nudity is disgusting, which is not God's intent.

Do not assume your young child will want to see pornography. It is common for young children to consider any form of sex, including pornography, as gross.

At the same time, do not assume your child will *not* want to see pornography. We never know when a child will become curious about sexuality.

When a child does show interest in pornography don't say things like "How could you?" or "Only bad kids look at pornography." All of us, including our children, are sexual beings and will eventually become attracted to sexual content. While pornography twists the concept of sexuality into something harmful, it is still a form of sex. We should not shame our children when they become interested in what God designed them to desire.

What You Should Do

Things we should do when addressing pornography at this age include the following:

- Make sure you don't display anger when talking about pornography. Try to smile now and then. Use a gentle tone of voice.
- Clearly define what you're talking about. There is a difference between art and pornography, which may be difficult for a young child to understand. We've already discussed modesty, and while we may not approve of classic nude statues or paintings, these are not examples of pornography. Pornography is any image, photo, video, or drawing of a nude person that focuses on private parts or touching private parts.
- Let them know that being curious about nudity is normal. Being curious is not bad, but pornography is not the way to learn about our bodies or about how sex works.
- Teach them that pornography is harmful. Their friends will likely tell them that pornography is fine or even good. You may be the only one telling them otherwise, so we can't hope someone else will explain this to them. We will discuss how to explain the dangers of pornography in the chapter Cleansing Conversations for Middle Children.

- Tell them that they will hear other kids talking about pornography. Using pornography is something that many people do, but that does not mean it is safe.
- Ask them to always tell you if they think they have seen pornography. We will discuss what to say in a moment if they have seen pornography.

Prepare Your Children for the Future

It is unfair to send a child into the world and expect them to avoid pornography without help. God has entrusted our children to us to protect them, and also prepare them for the future. We can teach our children some simple steps that will help them minimize the damage of exposure:

1. ***Close your eyes***. It sounds simple, and it is. Your child will see pornography—that is not in question. But when they do see it, they can close their eyes. If we drill into our kids' minds to close their eyes immediately when they see pornography, that will make it much more likely that they will. Otherwise, they will likely let their eyes linger, and quickly find it nearly impossible to look away.

2. ***Get away***. Teach children to make any excuse needed, or none at all, and get away from the source. Don't make them have to think about what to say to someone who shows them pornography; they can just leave.

3. ***Contact me*** (the parent). Teach your children that you are the person to go to immediately. You are the person to tell.

4. ***You will not be in trouble***. Your children need to know that it's safe to tell you when they have seen pornography, even if it was on purpose. You will need to live up to this promise. This is very important. If your child thinks he will get in trouble, he is not going to tell you. If he doesn't tell you, he will be left to try to resist pornography alone in the future—and he will fail.

When You Learn That Your Child Has Seen Pornography

When you discover your child has seen pornography, take a deep breath and pause. Tell yourself to remain calm, even if you feel yourself panicking. Smile. Hug your child. Once you've done that, here are nine more things you can do:

1. ***Thank your child for telling you.*** This assumes she told you rather than being caught by you or someone else. Make sure she understands that you are glad she came to you. If she was discovered, say something like, "You are not in trouble, but we need to talk." Remember, children must be assured their parents are safe to talk to; otherwise, they won't talk.

2. ***Find out what the child saw.*** Don't assume the worst; ask them to explain what they saw. Ask enough questions that you have a good idea of what they were exposed to.

3. ***Find out how it happened.*** Who else was involved? Where did it happen? Try not to sound accusative when asking for details. Your role is to sound caring and supportive, not angry.

4. ***Ask how they felt inside.*** We've discussed how important emotions are, and that our emotions are tightly connected to our sexuality. Give your child a chance to share how they felt, and then assure them it is okay to feel that way.

5. ***Ask if the images they saw are coming back to their minds.*** Children may be afraid to tell us this, so by asking we help them verbalize what they are experiencing. Assure them that there is nothing wrong with them if the images did return. Tell them they can talk to you any time the images come back, as that will help them feel better. If they do come to you, it's okay to help them find something fun to do to get the images out of their mind.

6. After discovering what has happened, ***discuss with the child how unrealistic and hurtful what they saw is***. Pornography typically portrays sex as an act of taking, aggression, or selfishness. This is not how God designed sex to be. Discuss how what your child saw is unlike how married people act together. Ask, how is what they saw unlike what people who care for each other do?

7. ***Ask if they have any questions for you.*** Seeing pornography will likely bring up many questions in a child's mind. Invite them to ask you. You might share your own first exposure to pornography and the questions it left you with, if you feel it's appropriate.

8. ***Give yourself and your child some time*** before talking about how to prevent future episodes. Discuss with your spouse what should be done going forward. This might mean not returning to certain places; being alone with specific people; or tightening safety measures on computers, mobile devices, TV, or game systems. There may need to be consequences, but those can wait until the child first feels supported and loved.

9. ***Pray with them.*** Demonstrate to them that we bring everything to God, even times we have been exposed to pornography. If your child purposefully looked up pornography, you can help them confess to God and assure them that Jesus forgives them. You could suggest they ask God to help them not keep remembering the images they saw so they don't stick with them.

These are cleansing conversations and actions you can have with your younger child. Your child is unique, as is the ideal timing of these conversations with your child. Be on the lookout for opportune teachable moments to have appropriate conversations about sexuality with them. If this feels like too much then select the conversations you feel most comfortable having with your children. Whatever you discuss with them will be helpful.

Parent-Child Activity: Option 1

Prepare your child to know what to do when they encounter pornography

Purchase a book to guide a conversation between you and your child about the reality of pornography, why it is harmful, and what they should do if they ever see it.

The best book to choose depends on the age of your child. The following are some recommendations:

- **Ages 6 and under**: *Good Pictures/Bad Pictures Jr.,* by Kristen Jensen
- **Ages 7-12**: *Good Pictures/Bad Pictures*, by Kristen Jensen
- **Ages 12 and up**: *How to Talk to Your Kids About Pornography*, by Educate & Empower Kids

When you order the book, estimate when it will arrive. Mark a date on your calendar when you plan to read the book with your child, selecting a date after the book should arrive.

Alternate Idea: Use a Resource to Start Conversation about Sex.

You could use the same idea to go through a resource together about sex. For resources on teaching appropriate information to your child about sex, see Appendix B and look for book and DVD resources listed under *God's Design for Sex*. Select one that matches the age of your child and the kinds of topics you want to teach now.

Parent-Child Activity: Option 2

Find out what questions your child has about sex.

This is a good idea if your child is between ages eight and twelve. This is not a time where you teach new information but a time to answer questions.

Here is one way this could work. One parent take one child on an outing. This could be the parent that the child seems to bring questions to the most or the parent of the same gender of the child.

The outing could be a short hike, a place that child likes to eat, a fishing trip, or to toss a ball around.

> **Parent Tip:** It is often easier for a child to talk about sex when they do not have to look directly at the parent. If you are on a hike or fishing, this works well because we do not typically face each other doing those things. If you take the child out to eat or anything that causes you to be face-to-face, you might have the conversation in the car or walk on the way to or from the place you are going.

When you are ready, ask the child the following. Change the wording to match how you normally talk.

1. Do you ever hear kids talking about sex?
2. What do they say?
3. I want you to know that you can ask me anything, even questions about sex or words you think might have something to do with sex.
4. When I was your age this is a question about sex I did not know the answer to (share the question but not the answer).
5. Do you have any questions I could help you with?

It is okay if your child does not have any questions. You have let them know that it is okay to ask you about sex. You have also demonstrated that you know what it is like to have questions about sex at their age. This is enough even if they ask you no questions.

If they do have questions about sex, answer them but do not go into a long discussion unless your child seems really interested. We do not want them to think that every question they ask about sex will turn into a lecture. Do your best to make this a positive experience.

6

Emotional Growth in Middle Children

Complex Emotions

Children roughly aged nine to twelve find themselves in more complex situations—which lead to more complex feelings. The Bible gives us an example of this. Samuel was a boy when we meet him in scripture. He had been given to a priest named Eli by his mother when Samuel was very young where the boy was to be trained to work in the temple.

It is likely that Samuel was between ages nine and twelve when he first heard the voice of God speaking directly to him. God told Samuel that Eli and his sons were going to be punished for some rather appalling behavior that Eli's sons were involved in, and which Eli had not corrected. We can only imagine what kind of emotions filled young Samuel as he wondered how the man he served under would react to such news.

Samuel lay down until morning and then opened the doors of the house of the Lord. He was afraid to tell Eli the vision, but Eli called him and said, "Samuel, my son." Samuel answered, "Here I am." "What was it He said to you?" Eli asked. "Do not hide it from me. May God deal with you, be it ever so severely, if

> *you hide from me anything He told you."*[28]
> *—The Prophet Samuel*

Even though this is a more complex situation than our children are likely to face, our middle children will likely face more complex problems than they are used to. Like Samuel, middle children are exposed to situations that cause more complex feelings than before. In addition, as children mature they realize that their parents can't protect them from everything and that not everyone can be trusted. This new reality leads to more difficult emotions.

As a result, we must talk with our middle children about emotions more often, and in more detail, than before. Our job as parents is to watch our middle children for signs that they need to talk through something that is bothering them, and to identify feelings they might have never had before.

Connecting Causes to Emotions

God wants us to learn from our emotions. Our middle childhood years are a time when children can begin to better understand the causes behind their emotions. Understanding the cause to an emotion gives clarity to a child about what he is really feeling.

Causes Clarify Emotions

Let's look at anger as an example. Anger is usually a sign that a deeper emotion lies beneath. When we see a child acting angry or grumpy, it means she has experienced something she doesn't like, but anger alone tells us nothing more. We need to help an angry child analyze what happened recently that might have caused her to feel angry, so she can uncover why she is angry. We can do this by asking questions.

Did someone make fun of her? If so, what does she feel beneath the anger? Does she feel hurt, rejected, or maybe even lonely?

Did she fail at something important to her? If so, she might feel ashamed or inadequate or like she is a failure as a person.

---

[28] 1 Samuel 3:15–17 (NIV)

Is she just really tired? Has she been pushed beyond what she feels she can do, and is reacting in anger instead of admitting to feeling overwhelmed?

Did she do something wrong and her anger is hiding the fear of getting caught? Does she actually feel guilty but wants to avoid that emotion?

Is she afraid of something? Some children do not want to admit to feeling afraid, and in trying to hide from fear, anger comes out instead.

We eventually want to train our children to stop and ask themselves why they feel the way they do. Until they learn how to do this, we are the ones who have to stop them and ask them to think about what caused them to feel a certain way. We then help them clarify what they really feel. Instead of anger or sadness, for example, their true emotions could be rejection, loneliness, failure, shame, inadequacy, feeling overwhelmed, fear, or guilt.

This skill of connecting an event to a resulting emotion is not something that middle children will master before their teen years. However, our middle-aged children can make significant progress, which will benefit them significantly when they are teenagers. Children who do not begin to identify causes of their feelings and learn to clarify what they actually feel before reaching age thirteen have much more difficulty managing the sexual feelings that come with puberty.

Reacting to Emotions

Once our children know what they are feeling and why, we can help them know how best to react to that emotion. Without help, middle children may try to distract themselves from negative emotions to mask a feeling they don't like or that feels threatening. A child might mask a feeling by turning on the TV, entering the artificial world of social media, becoming angry, isolating from others, or seeking out pornography or sexual stimulation.

The likelihood that a child will use one of these forms of escape is dependent on a number of factors. The closer a child gets to puberty, the more hormones play into the allure of sexual stimulation. We have to understand that sex hormones start taking effect approximately a year before any external signs are visible[29]. That means children feel the effects of puberty up to a year before external body changes begin.

In addition to puberty, early exposure to pornography can play a role in a child using pornography as an escape from negative emotions. This can happen quite young, and will continue until children learn to express their feelings to others instead of escaping.

Finally, children who have more trouble expressing their feelings will likely be more prone to using some form of escape to deal with feelings, no matter what age they are.

The Emotional Pain/Pornography Use Cycle

When our children experience a confusing or negative emotion, it causes them to feel discomfort. We are all familiar with that experience. If they do not know what to do with this discomfort, they will try to escape it in some way.

Pornography use and sexual stimulation can cause negative emotions to evaporate instantly in a child. Fantasy and lust in any form are great ways to escape negative emotions. Unfortunately, fantasy and lust also shut down positive emotions like feeling loved and understood. While sexual stimulation may feel a little like being loved and understood, there is no real person loving or understanding. We call this simulation of feeling loved "false intimacy."

False intimacy of this kind brings sensations and excitement to take the place of the paralyzed emotions within us. Unfortunately, not long after the sexual stimulation wears off, it is common for the child to feel shame over what he or she has done. Finally, the original negative emotions rush back in, because they were never resolved but only avoided for a time. The child ends up back where he started, with a painful emotion but now shame is added, making it even worse.

---

[29] Child Development Institute. (2005) Retrieved from: http://www.childdevelopmentinfo.com

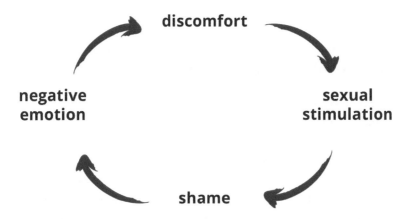

Because of the hyper-sexualized culture we live in, more and more children are becoming prey to false intimacy. We want our children not to fear negative emotions, and to know how to talk through them with others instead. At this age, parents must step in when we see our children feeling dejected, and encourage them.

> *But encourage each other daily, as long as it is still called "Today," so that none of you may be hardened by sin's deceitfulness.[30]*
> *—Unknown New Testament Author*

Emotional pain from relationships can be the most difficult for all of us, including children. Some children, by nature, have the ability to risk pursuing relationships even after experiencing relational pain. Other children shut down after experiencing relational rejection. They become emotionally numb, unwilling to risk entering into new relationships. They seek to control pain and pleasure in their lives by burying their emotions deep inside. These children are at a higher risk of pursuing sexual behaviors or pornography to hide from those feelings.

How We Can Help

Children aged nine to twelve identify emotions the same way younger children do. If you have not yet used a feelings chart from

---

[30] Hebrews 3:13 (NIV)

Appendix A, it's not too late to start. We can still discuss feelings of characters in movies or stories as before. We definitely should be sharing our own feelings on a regular basis, to model for our children how to identify their own feelings.

Be With Them

Once a child identifies a negative emotion, the first thing we can do is simply be with them. We are their primary source of comfort and sense of stability. When we are with them, they feel a sense that we are sharing their pain—which, as any parent knows, we usually are. Yes, we may have to put aside something else we were doing, but our children need us, and they need to know that their feelings are very important to us.

Allow Emotions to Come Out

It is fine, even good, to cry along with our children at times. We should not tell them to stop crying, unless the crying has changed from sorrow to throwing a fit. We should not say things like, "Don't be sad." We should not give them candy or a treat to make them "feel better." These words and actions send the message that negative feelings are bad, are to be avoided, and should not be expressed—all of which are completely false.

Address the Cause

We might then encourage our child to do something that addresses the cause of their emotion. If they feel lonely or rejected, perhaps we can help them set up a time to spend with a close friend. Even if that time is a few days away, this is still teaching a child to proactively care for his or her emotional wellbeing. If he feels like a failure after repeated attempts at something he is not good at, perhaps we can encourage him to find something else he enjoys that he is better at. The goal is not to come up with something that immediately reverses the negative emotion but that helps him in the long run.

However, often the only thing that needs to happen is that your child needs someone to talk to and comfort them. I remember my son being around ten, flopping down on the couch and saying. "I don't know why, but I just feel sad today." This was one of the first times he had appropriately expressed a feeling on his own. I could tell he was trying to figure out why he was sad but couldn't. I realized at that moment the more important thing was for him to get a positive result from trying to express his sadness. So I chose not to drill him about what might be causing him to be sad or what a more accurate word might be to describe what he was feeling. Instead, I just sat by him, put my arm around him, and said I was glad he told me. We just sat together for a while and he soon felt better.

This isn't about playing psychologist to our children; it's about being with them as they try to navigate their feelings. It's about helping them stay in the real world instead of escaping into fantasy. Sometimes we'll have deep discussions with our kids about feelings; other times we'll just sit together on the couch. Either way, our children are learning helpful ways to deal with painful feelings.

Emotional Natives

There is a side effect of teaching young children to be emotionally aware that is only fair to mention at this point. If we do a good job of helping our children achieve emotional awareness in their younger years, they are likely to surpass us as middle or older children. The way this childhood skill manifests itself can feel disturbing to parents, but is actually a good thing.

Most of us had no such emotional training as children, and we are still trying to figure out our own emotions as adults. When we teach children how to deal with feelings starting when they're very young, some of them get really good at it. It becomes their native language when we are still speaking emotions as a second language. Then they become our teachers—and sometimes that isn't all that fun for the parent. This is how it looked in our family.

A Story of Emotionally Aware Children

I came home from work one day, upset about something. I was grumpy and speaking curtly to my family. My daughter, at all of eleven, said very patiently and calmly, "Dad, it looks like you had a bad day. It's okay to be upset, but don't be mad at us, because we didn't do anything."

I am human, and I will tell you that it took all the self-control I could muster not to react very inappropriately to my daughter pointing out my poor behavior. I felt a flash of anger at first, and then realized she was actually right. As I stood frozen in place, trying to understand what had just happened, I finally realized the reason she was right is because my wife and I had apparently done a good job teaching her how people are supposed to deal with emotions. I can tell you that was one confusing soup of emotions, with anger, embarrassment, and pride all mixed together. I had to go to my room and compose myself.

It can feel disrespectful when our child points out our flaws, even if they are trying to help. Nonetheless, it is entirely appropriate for a child to ask anyone—even a parent—to not impose their emotions on the child. Once I got over my initial reaction, I was proud of my daughter for learning so well what I had been teaching her.

I wish I could tell you that this was an isolated incident. Instead, on repeated occasions over several years, one child or the other would ask my wife or I to get our emotions under control and react appropriately. They said it nicer than that, but they didn't mince words either. My wife and I have learned to laugh and realize that our children have simply passed us by in this area. I should clarify they were *sometimes* better than us. Each of our children were their own emotional messes at times during their teen years . . . but we'll get to that later.

Parent-Child Activity: Option 1

Helping a Child Clarify an Emotion

Depending on the age of your child, this may be a good exercise. It will require you to watch your child carefully this week and look for an opportunity. This is a teachable moment exercise, not something you can mark on your calendar to do.

Instructions:

1. Watch your child this week and observe times when he or she seems to be mad, sad, or happy.

2. When you see one of these emotions come to the surface, stop what you are doing.

3. Sit down with him or her and ask how he or she is feeling. If they say, "mad, sad, or happy" do not try to clarify that feeling further yet.

4. Ask why they think they feel this way—that is, what happened to cause him or her to feel like this. Work with them to find the cause of their feeling.

5. If they still cannot identify a feeling beyond, "mad, sad, or happy" go to Appendix A and look at the *Complex Feelings* chart. Work together to try to find a more specific word to describe what they are feeling. Remember, the feelings chart is only a partial list of feelings.

6. Think of a similar situation in your life when you felt the same feeling, and share that story with your child of what happened and how you felt.

7. If your child seems open to more discussion, ask them what are good things to do when they feel this way.

8. Share what you do when you feel this way.

9. Thank him or her for telling you their feelings.

Parent-Child Activity: Option 2

Model Clarifying Emotions

Depending on the age of your child, this may be a good exercise. The goal is for you to use your own story to illustrate how emotions work and how we can clarify what we are really feeling.

Instructions:

1. Think of a time when something happened that created a strong negative emotion in you.
2. If you were to categorize your general reaction, was it closer to mad, sad, or happy?
3. Determine what feeling or emotion most clearly describes how you felt when this event happened? Use the feelings chart in Appendix A if you need to.
4. Now prepare to share this with your child.
5. Pick a time to talk with your child when they are not too busy. Make sure they are not tired or sleepy first.
6. Sit down with them and tell them this is a homework assignment for a book you are reading that you need their help with.
7. Tell them about the event that happened.
8. Tell them if this made you feel generally mad, sad, or happy.
9. Then tell them how you figured out which deeper emotion you really felt: such as shame, failure, insulted, disrespected, or so on.
10. Then tell your assignment was to ask them to help you decide what would be a good way to deal with this feeling if it happens again. Point them away from any suggestion based on revenge or fixing the initial event.
11. Talk through a few possible things you could do next time.
12. If they seem open, ask if they have ever experienced something like what you experienced and felt.
13. Thank them for their help. Do not overdo trying to apply your situation to theirs. They can figure that out on their

own, unless they specifically ask for your advice on something.

7

Cleansing Conversations
for Middle Children

Starting the Conversation

Our children have lots of questions, confusion, and possibly hurts when it comes to sexuality by ages nine through twelve. By this time they are more aware of sexuality, though they don't understand the intertwining of all the emotions, relationships, spirituality, and physical aspects involved. Some children have been called names that are tied to some form of sexuality. Hormones can kick in during the later part of this stage. Some may have experienced unkind or unwanted sexual interest from peers. Middle children need help working through situations like this that are happening to them and around them.

By age nine children are old enough to have more in-depth conversations about sex and even sexual feelings. Some children come to us directly with questions. Others will feel nervous and keep quiet. In the same manner that Jesus pursues us, we should engage our children, to help them through any confusion they may have. If we wait for them to ask, we cheat them out of helpful information and leave them vulnerable to the sexual influence of others.

What we don't Want to Happen

I remember one father telling me that he knew it was time to give his almost-nine-year-old son more information about sex. He had bought *God's Design for Sex, Books 1-4*, mentioned in Appendix B, and read the first two with his son when he was younger. For weeks he told me that he was going to get to the next book soon. Then one day he picked up the family Internet tablet, and found the browser history full of hardcore videos depicting sex. He talked with his son, who admitted he had looked those videos up. Then his son said, "Remember that set of books about sex and we read the first ones when I was little? I think it's time for the next one. I want to know some things."

If we don't answer our kids' questions about sex they will go looking for answers on their own. Our kids may not tell us they have questions, but that doesn't mean we should be silent. We are the parents, and as scary as it is, we need to take the initiative to talk about sex.

What we do Want to Happen

Another father came to me one day and said he had planned a time to talk to his almost-nine-year-old son about sex. I wasn't sure why he was telling me, other than perhaps to gather his courage to follow through. The next week the same father came up to me with a big smile on his face. He said he took his son on a father-son trip, where he taught him age appropriate information about sex and answered all his questions. He told me his son's response was, "Thanks for telling me. I feel special because now I know stuff that other kids don't, and I know the right answers."

The two stories above are real and happened just as I explained. I'm not making things up. They also happened within a couple of months of each other, which made them stand out in my mind and end up being repeated in this book. They do paint a rather stark picture of how our parenting choices can affect our children.

When we are feeling nervous about having our next conversation about sex, we can ask ourselves, "Which of the above stories do I want my child to share?" Our nervousness cannot dictate what we tell our children. The stakes are too high.

Some middle children are not so eager to bring their questions to parents. Such children may never ask where babies come from, or act squeamish during appropriate mentioning of body parts. It can be tempting, and is certainly easier, for a parent to simply remain silent with a child like this. However, these children still need to be educated with correct information, and that won't happen without parent intervention.

My own son and daughter were both rather uncomfortable when we first started teaching them about sex. By the third conversation, however, they each started to ask questions and were comfortable talking about sexuality. It's okay if it takes a child a while to open up.

The Single Parent

Topics about sex are awkward for any parent, but single parents tend to feel less comfortable discussing them with children of the opposite gender. It gets a little tougher when puberty is part of the discussion. But we want you to know that it is not true that a single parent cannot discuss sexual topics with a child of the opposite gender. A single parent may choose to enlist the help of other trusted adults, but there is still a lot a single parent can do on his or her own.

Remember that none of us are alone. We have the Holy Spirit to guide us and to open the hearts of our children. We don't need to do this under our own power. We can ask for His help, and help will be given.

Second, while it is not customary in our culture, adults and children of opposite genders can discuss anything, even related to sex. Girls experience menstruation and boys experience wet dreams. Both are embarrassing and awkward to talk about, but if the child is willing, it is okay to discuss with a parent of the opposite sex. Children can be remarkably willing to open up when they see that the parent is also willing.

If a single parent decides an outside voice is needed, they can seek help from trusted adults in their church or community. But never feel paralyzed or unable to broach any topic if you feel it needs to be addressed before you can find someone to help. The following is a real-life example:

> *I am a single mother with two boys. They see their father only occasionally, as he does not live in our state. I have to handle this alone. When my oldest boy brought up masturbation, I wasn't sure I was even allowed to talk to him about it. I had never considered talking to my son about such a thing, but because he was asking me, I just did the best I could. It was really awkward, but we got through it. Later, I asked a man I trust what to say to a boy about masturbation. He gave me several helpful thoughts, which I shared with my oldest son later. Now, when I don't know what to say, I ask men I trust, but I do all the talking to my boys. It seems to be working.*

There is no prescription for single-parent families, but there is no single prescription for multi-parent families either. We all have to find what works for us. None of us should feel alone in our parenting. We have a community and God to rely on for help.

Teaching God's Design for Sex

When our children become aware that sex is something that happens between a husband and wife, we need to give them more information than the difference in male and female sex organs. We also need to go beyond how babies are conceived and born. Here are some conversations that middle children will eventually need to have with you, so that they can understand what God made sex for.

These are topics we discussed in chapter 3, *Sexual Wholeness*, but we will take time here to help you know how to convey this information to your children.

God Created Sex

Children need to know that sex was God's idea. This will help some children let go of the incorrect idea that sex is somehow bad or dirty. When sex is used as God designed it to be used, it is a good and even a sacred act.

Sex Unites Us

You can explain to your child that God designed sex to act as an emotionally bonding agent between husband and wife. Every time a husband and wife have sex, something happens in their brains that make them want to stay together. In a way, sex is like glue in that it makes us stick together.

You can tell your children that this is what the Bible is talking about when it says, "the two shall become one" (Matthew 19:5). It means the two begin to feel like one, through the process of sex.

Sex is for Husbands and Wives

Sex, in a loving context, causes the man and woman involved to develop a bond that causes them to want to stay together. God created sex to have a powerful purpose in making a husband and wife want to stay together. Therefore, we reserve sex for the one we wish to be united to for life.

God asks us not to do sexual things with anyone other than the person we marry because of what sex can do in those situations. When used in a way other than what it was created for, it can cause us to feel bonded to people we are not supposed to be bonded to. This is not like a bond of friendship, but a deeper emotional attraction that is designed only for husband and wife. We don't want to have that kind of feeling for people we will not marry. When we do, we continue to have those feelings even when we end up marrying someone else later.

Jesus Himself tells us not to do sexual things with people we are not married to. The word "fornication" means doing sexual things with someone we are not married to.

> *For from within, out of the heart of men, proceed the evil thoughts, fornications, thefts, murders, adulteries, deeds of coveting and wickedness, as well as deceit, sensuality, envy, slander, pride and foolishness. All these evil things proceed from within and defile the man.[31]*
> *—Jesus*

---

[31] Mark 7:21-23 (NASB)

You will have to be careful and explain only as much of this as your child is able to comprehend, which depends on their age and maturity. However, when a child asks, "What is sex for?" we need to include that it is for marriage and to bond a husband and wife to whatever degree our child can comprehend.

God Made Sex to Be Enjoyed

The Bible says sex is to be enjoyed in marriage. Children deserve to know this. "Rejoice in the wife of your youth,"[32] is one such passage. The Song of Solomon is a celebration of marital sex. Sex was intended by God to be enjoyed to the fullest in marriage. Our children need to know this.

As a result, our children should not be afraid to look forward to the day they are married and begin sexual activity. Because sex is good and created by God, it is okay for them to look forward to it.

Sex is to be Selfless

Children need to understand that sex is not something we "get" from someone else. Almost everything they see or hear from the world's point of view is about taking or getting sex from someone. This is a very unhealthy viewpoint of sex and not something that acts in a bonding or uniting way in marriage.

Sex is something we offer to our spouse, not demand or take. Putting our spouse first sexually is part of the overall message of Christ to put the needs of others before our own.

Sex Is Spiritual

Children should learn that sex is not something we do apart from God. From a spiritual perspective, sex is the most intimate expression of marital love. It is an experience reserved for a husband and wife. Sex is also compared in the Bible to meeting God. This makes the action of sex something extremely special and holy.

No part of our lives is intended to be outside the sphere of our spirituality, including sex. God designed sex, and it is a holy act. We cannot hide sex from God, and He doesn't want us to. Sex is an act

---

[32] Proverbs 5:18b (NASB)

we partake in with our spouse in the presence of God Himself. God blesses such sexual union and celebrates with us.

Waiting for Sex

Because it is a long time before children will be old enough to marry, they should know it is not helpful to obsess about sex—that would be frustrating. Sex is not unique in that it is something they need to wait for. It is good if they want to drive a car on the road, but twelve-year-olds that are "more grown up" are still not allowed to drive. Obsessing about wanting to drive a car will only make them irritated and miss out on other joys of life in the meantime. The same is true about waiting to marry or to be old enough to work at a bank.

We can tell our children that we are glad they want to drive a car, have a job, get married, and have sex. Those are all good things to long for, but we must also teach our children to wait for them and enjoy the life God gives us in the meantime.

It could be helpful if you can think of some things, other than sex, that you really wanted to do as a child that you had to wait for. You could explain how you managed to wait and how glad you were when you were finally old enough to do whatever it was you were waiting for.

Readdressing Pornography

We need to address pornography again when children get older, as it is likely that their curiosity about pornography will have increased by ages nine to twelve. We can teach middle children that pornography can be attractive because it depicts sex, and we are designed to be drawn to sex, as we get older.

But we also need to point out that pornography is a broken form of sexuality. Pornography is not real sex, so it cannot provide any of the benefits of real sex. It is harmful to the person being depicted and to the brains of people indulging in it. Pornography only leaves us isolated and lonely in the end. Our children won't know this and may have a hard time understanding how true this is. We will list some of the ways pornography has been proven to harm us in a moment.

A Different Form of Pornography

Pornography that exists today is not the same as what we called pornography in our childhood. Some of our generation only had access to magazines. Others had access to the Internet, but it was slow and pornography came in the form of photos or very grainy animated clips that took time to download. Today, children have access to instant downloading, high-resolution videos of sexual encounters of unlimited variety and endless supply. Children don't need to hide a magazine under a mattress where it might be found; they can get it from any device that accesses the Internet, and many are smart enough not to get caught.

We should briefly review a couple of differences between modern pornography and what we may have had access to when we were children. First of all, it is far more difficult to resist once a child has been exposed to it. The endless novelty of motion and sound are significantly more engaging than what came before.

Second, there is a rapidly growing amount of research demonstrating how Internet pornography is particularly harmful to children. Consumption of modern Internet pornography has been linked to changes in the structure of the human brain.[33] As a result, frequent pornography use by adolescents has shown to cause loneliness and depression,[34] lower levels of self-esteem,[35] and uncertainty about their own sexuality,[36] to name just a few.

[33.] S. Kühn S and J. Gallinat, "Brain Structure and Functional Connectivity Associated with Pornography Consumption: The Brain on Porn," JAMA Psychiatry 71:7 (July 1, 2014): 827–34

[34.] Michele L. Ybarra and Kimberly J. Mitchell, "Exposure to Internet Pornography among Children and Adolescents: A National Survey," CyberPsychology & Behavior 8 (2005): 479

[35.] Todd G. Morrison et al., "Exposure to Sexually Explicit Material and Variations in Body Esteem, Genital Attitudes, and Sexual Esteem among a Sample of Canadian Men," The Journal of Men's Studies 14 (2006): 216–17

[36] J. Peter and P. M. Valkenburg, "Adolescents' Exposure to Sexually Explicit Internet Material, Sexual Uncertainty, and Attitudes toward Uncommitted Sexual Exploration: Is There a Link?" Communication Research, 35:5 (2008): 595

The pornographic material our children have access to is a much more dangerous animal than what we grew up with.

Helping Middle Children Avoid Pornography

Children who are approaching or new to puberty will need a lot of help from parents restricting access to sources of pornography, due to their low level of willpower (something we will discuss more in chapter eight). Giving a child this age a smart phone, music device that connects to the Internet, or Internet tablet is a very bad idea. Children below age 14 do not have the emotional skills to resist the allure of pornography and other unhealthy content online. Their curiosity is simply too great.

Before you think this is too restrictive, you should know that Bill Gates did not allow his children to have cell phones until they were fourteen and strictly limited screen and video game time.[37] Steve Jobs prohibited his kids from using an iPad at all, even though he helped create it[38]. These men knew what was online that their kids did not have the maturity to avoid.

We will discuss later why adolescents are particularly vulnerable to pornography and have a low ability to resist it. Right now let us consider some ways you can help them better resist something so alluring.

Tell Your Story First

We cannot possibly expect our children to tell us what they are experiencing and feeling if we won't tell them the same. By this age, it is very important for parents to tell their own stories of exposure to pornography. This does a couple of things. First, it helps our children know that we do understand how they feel, because we've been there. Even if they are not attracted to pornography yet, they will be, and it will help them to know we understand what that feels like. Second, it helps children believe we are serious when we say it

---

[37] Chris Weller, "Bill Gates & Steve Jobs Raised Their Kids Tech-Free", Business Insider, Oct 24, 2017

[38] Nick Bilton, "Steve Jobs Was a Low-Tech Parent", The New York Times, Sep 10, 2014

is safe for them to tell us when they slip and look at pornography. If we share first, they are much more likely to share later.

I told my son about my first exposure to pornography when he was eleven. If it were today, I would probably tell him by age eight. I told my son that when I was nine a boy my age showed me pornography at a sleepover. My friend had just found his father's pornographic magazine stash and wanted to show it to us. I had no idea this was going to happen when I accepted his invitation to sleep over. He'd invited another boy, so there were three of us. The magazines had nude images of women and a few of men. I was stunned and didn't really know what to think, but I wanted to be cool, so I didn't object as the other two put more and more magazines in front of me. Some of the pictures seemed gross to me, but others made me feel excited.

In the following days and weeks, I had all kinds of confused feelings. I knew my parents would not want me to see what I had seen, so I felt ashamed that I had allowed myself to look at those kinds of pictures. When I went to church, I felt God trying to talk to me about what I'd seen, and I thought He was mad at me, so I didn't talk to Him about it. I kept everything a secret even though I had lots of questions and jumbled up feelings.

I continued to tell my son that later, when I was married, I learned that the way they showed the men and women in the magazines is not really how husbands and wives treat each other. Pornography didn't help me understand real sex, and what it showed me was not true at all about sex. I didn't know how to act when I was married, and that made it hard for his mother and I for a while. Again, I told my son that I wished that someone had taught me what real sex was like between married people, so I didn't stay confused so long.

How much to share with a child depends on how old the child is and how much he or she already knows about sex. I would try to include the following when you tell your story about your first exposure to pornography:

- how old you were
- how it happened
- a very general description of what you saw

- how you felt when you saw it
- how you felt after—perhaps including any secrecy and shame, as well as a desire to see more
- any problems it caused for you later on
- how unrealistic you discovered it is

The last point above is important. Our children need to understand that what pornography portrays has little resemblance to what we experience in real life.

Explaining How Pornography Is Harmful

Pornography that exists today is quite harmful, particularly to children. Some children will naturally sense that pornography is harmful. This does not mean that it will be easy for them to resist it. Others may have a harder time understanding why something so attractive is harmful. Either way, children should understand how pornography harms them; otherwise they may see it as just another rule parents give children that don't make sense.

Do not talk obsessively with your child about the dangers of pornography, however. In doing so you can create curiosity and make them want to go see for themselves what the fuss is all about. Remember we want to talk more about the positive aspects of sex, not the negative. Tell enough that your child understands the danger but no so much that they get tired of hearing you and begin to ignore you.

Here are some things you may consider telling your child to help them understand why pornography is harmful. You do not have to share all of this at once, and you do not even have to share all of it. All we need to do is make sure our children understand that pornography is harmful, not make them fear it is a monster out to get them.

Pornography is harmful because:

- It is harmful to the people who are being filmed. In many cases they are being forced to participate and are being treated like slaves. They are often forced to use drugs to be able to look happy when they are not. Afterward, the people who perform pornography are left feeling deep shame at what they did and the fact so many will see it. Pornography is extremely cruel to those who are forced to act it out.

- Prolonged use of Internet pornography causes physical changes in the brain of the viewer. These changes result in: reduced emotional bonds with real people, attention deficit, loss of willpower, social anxiety, decreased satisfaction with real sex, erectile dysfunction in young adult males, negative body image, increased impulsivity in all areas of life, loneliness, depression, low self-worth.[39]

- It gives an unrealistic view of relating. This is not how people relate to each other in real life.

- It gives unrealistic views of sex. This is not how real people treat each other sexually. This is not what to expect in marriage.

- It portrays people treating each other like objects. Treating people like objects will drive people away from us, not help us make friends.

- It teaches that sex is selfish and about getting what I want. The purpose of sex is for two people to share a deep form of intimacy. We can't learn that from pornography.

- It makes us ignore more important things we should be doing. It makes us want to lock ourselves away from others and spend hours in isolation.

- In the long run, it makes us lonely. Healthy sex makes us feel loved, but pornography makes us feel isolated and alone.

- It can be very difficult to stop, because it is very addictive. The unlimited supply of endlessly new sexual images causes our brains to constantly want more, even though it is isolating us from friends and family.

- All negative effects of pornography listed above impact children under age 25 more than older adults.[40] This is due

---

[39] Your Brain on Porn, "Brain Studies on Porn Users," (2014) http://yourbrainonporn.com/brain-scan- studies-porn-users (accessed July 13, 2016).

[40] Frances E. Jensen with Amy Ellis Nutt, The Teenage Brain: A Neuroscientist's Survival Guild to Raising Adolescents and Young Adults, (New York: Harper Collins, 2015); Doremus-Fitzwater, Elena I. Varlinskaya, and Linda P. Spear, "Motivational Systems in Adolescence: Possible Implications for Age Differences in Substance Abuse and Other Risk-Taking Behaviors," Brain and Cognition 71, no. 1 (2010):114– 123.

to the fact that the brain is still developing and is more susceptible to outside influences.

To help a child understand the concept of something being attractive, dangerous, and addictive, you might refer to C. S. Lewis's book *The Lion, The Witch, and the Wardrobe.* In chapter four, Edmund tastes an enchanted Turkish Delight. He discovers he can never get enough Turkish Delight; he becomes obsessed, and gets his siblings and himself in serious trouble as a result. This is a very accurate analogy to what happens to our minds when we are exposed to the modern-day form of pornography.

Electronic Devices and Middle Children

We should absolutely install *accountability/monitoring software* on every Internet device our children have access to. This tells us when our children have given into curiosity and looked at something inappropriate. The point isn't to catch them doing something wrong, but to know when we need to have a particular discussion. Software helps us know what our children saw. We then can ask, "How was that an unhealthy view of human sexuality? How was that not a good way for people to treat each other sexually?" No accountability software is foolproof, but it is unwise to use that as an excuse not to use it in your home.

It is best to not allow a pre-teen to have a cell phone or tablet with Internet access. If you decide to do that, you should make sure they don't take Internet devices behind closed doors. Allowing an older child or teenager to take Internet devices into the bathroom or behind a closed bedroom door asks for more self-control than our children have. We should not shame them but say something like, "You are becoming an adult, with adult hormones, which are too strong for us to resist while taking a peek at pornography in a private place."

Of course, we can only use this method if we are willing to live by the same house rules. If we don't want our kids taking phones and tablets to the bathroom, we shouldn't either. A child can internalize, "I am an adult now, so I don't take my devices behind closed doors," instead of, "My parents are treating me like a kid and won't let me take my phone into the bathroom/bedroom." Not that there won't be any battles, but this certainly makes it easier.

Remember that many TVs and video games have access to the Internet that cannot be monitored by the same software that works on computers and phones. Use parental controls to help when possible. Always know what your children are doing with video games and through the TV.

Come back to this topic from time to time.

Our children's attraction to pornography can change quite suddenly. We cannot assume that how they felt two months ago is what they feel this month. We can simply ask if anything has happened where they saw pornography since we talked last. Remind them we want to know if that ever happens. Maybe we can tell our children another of our stories of exposure from time to time. The goal is to help them feel safe for when the time does come when they are exposed to pornography.

Positive Gender Messages

Affirming our children with positive gender messages is incredibly important. By around age eleven or twelve, and increasing in early teens, children begin to ponder who they are. While gender is certainly not the most important part of our identity, it is still part of who we are. Our current culture would tell our children that it is up to them to decide who they are. While on the surface this may sound like a freeing approach, it actually adds stress to a child.

We can help our children understand that we do not choose our identity. Our identity is bestowed upon us by someone in authority. God is the first authority to bestow identity upon us:

> *God created man in His own image, in the image of God He created him; male and female He created them.*[41]

Being male or female is part of our image, and the first thing God bestows on us. It does not give a child comfort to be told they

---

[41] Genesis 1:27 (NASB)

must determine which gender they want to be—it lays an enormous burden on them! That is a huge responsibility and far more stress than any child was meant to handle. God already gave each of us this part of our identity.

What It Means to Be Male or Female

Notice that God made us in his image, *male and female.* Think about what this passage is saying. God's character is found in both male and female traits. It would appear that within God are characteristics of both males and females.

When we as parents get too hung up on how boys or girls are supposed to act, this can end up stressing our kids out rather than giving them comfort in who they are. God is nurturing, so it should be perfectly fine for a man or boy to have a nurturing nature. God can be strong and forceful, so it should be fine for a girl or woman to have a forceful personality. We are all made in his image. If we're going to affirm our children in the gender in which they were born, we will need to do so in such a way that allows them to express themselves the way God made them. We can affirm a gentle son in his masculinity as much as the roughhousing son. We can affirm an aggressive daughter in her femininity as much as a delicate daughter. We must provide for them a sense of security in the unique way God made them to be.

Each parent has a role to play in helping their children feel confident with their gender. Both boys and girls need a father's words and a mother's words. The father, however, has a very important, God-given role in validating a son's masculinity and a daughter's femininity. My counselor friend Ann Martin talks about how the father's role in affirming gender plays out for boys and girls:

> *The dads really have a big role in their daughter and son's self-worth. It's a huge responsibility and I truly believe it's how God designed it. He asked us to call Him "father" and I believe its part of extending that. Boys need to know that they're okay, that they're good enough, and that they've made the mark of masculinity. Oftentimes, I see adult men come into my counseling office, and they are struggling with self-worth or they've become workaholics. In these*

cases, I often find they never got their dad's approval growing up. They still want to hear their dad say, "Hey, I approve of you!" Boys need that from their dad.

Daughters need to know that they are captivating. They need to know that they are pretty. Most little girls will dress up and twirl around and ask, "Aren't I pretty?" They want to know that they're attractive. They also want to know that they are smart—they are good at things, and they are really looking for this affirmation from their dad.

I remember when my youngest was trying some clothes on and she came up to me and I said, "That looks really cute!" Then she showed her dad and she came back to me and said, "Dad really liked it!" It was more important what he said than what I said.[42]

The mother has an important role in affirming gender as well. The mother is typically the parent who proclaims when a girl has become a woman. Similar to the father with a daughter, the mother declares the son attractive and desirable to women. As my own son grew older, he cared more and more what my wife thought about the clothes he wore than what I thought. Because she was a woman, he wanted to know what a woman thought of him. In this way, each parent plays a critical role in affirming our children in their gender.

The Single Parent

We do not want to leave out single parents in this discussion about positive gender messages. A single mother can only go so far in proclaiming her son a man. A single father can only be so convincing telling his daughter she is a woman when he's never been one. This is where the community that God intended for us comes in. Single parents can develop a network of adults, who assist them in speaking masculinity or femininity into their children. A single mother can enlist the help of safe men in her church to speak into the lives of their sons. A single father can do the same with the help of other women.

---

[42] Ibid

All children do best when multiple adults affirm them in their gender and identity in Christ. Single parent or not, we should all seek out other positive adult influences for our children. God never intended for our children to be hidden away in our homes. He built his church to be a community and extended family, even for our children.

We are in fact all one family, as Jesus explained:

> *Looking about at those who were sitting around Him, He said, "Behold My mother and My brothers! For whoever does the will of God, he is My brother and sister and mother".*[43]

Finally, we cannot forget that God is the Father of all. For single mothers, this can be a helpful reminder to their children. Children have an eternal Father who is ready to listen to them at any time. God will affirm children who come to Him. Trust that God will do this, and encourage your children to spend time alone with their Father in heaven.

The More Important Identity

Our children live in a very different world than we grew up in. They hear sexual misinformation every day, including as it relates to gender. Putting too much weight on gender as an identity is not always helpful. After all, God designed us to have a more important primary identity.

God never wanted us to feel anxiety about who we are. His message to us is clear—above all, we are his children:

> *for in Him we live and move and exist, as even some of your own poets have said, **"For we also are His children." Being then the children of God**, we ought not to think that the Divine Nature is like gold or silver or stone, an image formed by the art and thought of man.*[44]
> —*The Apostle Luke*

Note that Luke explains to us that our image has nothing to do with anything we have done or made. We do not have to build our

---

[43] Mark 3:34–35 (NASB)
[44] Acts 17:28–29 (NASB) emphasis added

own image. It was God who made us, not ourselves. Our children are sons and daughters of God. They are sisters and brothers of Jesus. They are royalty of the universe, not by any human effort, but through God's.

This is in direct contrast to what the world is telling our children. Our children are told they have to discover, even decide on their own, who they are. If a child is expected to decide who they are all on their own, they could be left unsure of their choice the rest of their lives. A life of uncertainty in identity brings instability, not freedom. God, on the other hand, has a permanent and unchanging identity for our children.

*He [Jesus] came to His own, and those who were His own did not receive Him. But as many as received Him, to them He gave the right to become **children of God**, even to those who believe in His name.*[45]
—The Apostle John

God did not abandon us to create or discover our identity. He gave us an identity as His children that is an anchor amidst the uncertainty of our culture. We can help our children understand and own their identity. Their identity is not built on something as fragile as a personality type, or as impermanent as our culture considers sexual identity.

As children of God, our children can know that they do not need to worry about their future; it is secure in the hands of the Father, as long as they remain connected to the identity He provides. This is a safe identity, not one that might cause them harm.

"For I know that plans I have for you," declares the Lord, "plans to prosper you and not to harm you, plans to give you hope and a future".[46]
—The Prophet Jeremiah

---

[45] John 1:11–12 (NASB) emphasis added
[46] Jeremiah 29:11, (NIV)

We can teach our children that above all, their identity is rooted in being children of God. Any other form of identity pales in importance.

Relationships

It is typical for children to want to develop closer relationships with the opposite gender by age twelve, if not before. Parents do not need to feel alarmed when a child this age comes home and says, "I like a boy," or "I have a girlfriend now." At this age, those words typically do not mean what we think they mean.

When we hear a child use words similar to these we should ask them what they mean. What do they mean by "like someone" or "girlfriend/boyfriend?" How is that relationship different than other friends they have? What would they do that is different? If we ask these questions, we often find out that they simply mean they feel more interested in this person than they have felt before. Not all children will have such feelings at this age but some will. We might as well talk about them if they do.

Learning to be appropriately close emotionally with both genders is an important stage of development for this age. However, we should help them understand that this is still friendship. Our children may like someone of the opposite gender in a new way, but at this age, it is still friendship. Children need plenty of time to learn how to manage such relationships before moving into anything more serious. For more information on talking to children about relationships, see Appendix B and recommended resources on the topic.

Discussing relationships is not limited to opposite-gender friends. Same gender friends of this age may share sexual jokes or sexual information that is inaccurate and unhelpful. We need to ask what our children talk about with friends, and pointedly ask them about sexual conversations. While we have to be realistic and realize we can't completely protect our children from sexual misinformation, we can protect our children from going places where they are likely to be introduced to unhealthy views of sex. We don't want to become so restrictive that we don't allow our children to leave the house, but we can and should decide who is safe and unsafe for our children to spend time with.

We should not restrict our conversations about our children's friends to making sure that their friends are not introducing them to unhealthy sexual ideas. We should show a true interest in their friends and their world. This makes our children feel valued, which is critical to a lasting relationship with them.

Peer Pressure

God gave us families to use as assistance in resisting peer pressure. Families are our tightest community unit and are the place to diffuse the power of peer pressure. Peer pressure can take the form of pressuring our child to look at a pornographic image or video, listen to a sexual joke, or send a sexually explicit text or photo to someone.

We can talk to our children about the danger of such behavior without overreacting. We can ask them if they see children pressuring other children to do inappropriate things. We can then ask if anyone has asked them to do any of these things. We should always share our experiences at their age as well.

The nice thing is there are really only two things a child this age needs to know in order to deal with peer pressure. When a friend tries to get them to participate in inappropriate sexual behavior they should 1) walk away, and 2) tell you as soon as possible. At ages nine to twelve our children don't need to know how to stand up to kids who are asking them to do inappropriate things. That's what the parent is for. At this age, the best thing a child can do is just leave.

Parent-Child Activity: Option 1

Explaining God's Purpose for Sex

If you think your child is old enough to know more than just the mechanics of sex, this might be your next conversation with them. Plan ahead and select a time when your child will not be distracted. You could even have this conversation while driving in the car. Or you could be seated somewhere and use the following as conversation notes.

Instructions:

1. Ask your child where sex came from. Ask them whose idea was sex in the first place. Guide the conversation to the conclusion that sex was God's idea.

2. Ask them if they have ever thought about sex being God's idea. Ask them what they think this must mean.

3. Ask them if they knew that God has another purpose for sex besides making babies. Tell them you would like to explain what that is.

4. Tell your child something to the effect of, "**God created sex just for husbands and wives to share.** He created us so that when we have sex, a chemical called 'oxytocin' is released in our brains. This happens to men and women. When that chemical is in our brain, it makes us feel strong attraction to the person we are with and it makes us feel emotionally close to them. **Sex creates the feeling of a special, very close bond with that person.**"

5. That may be all you need to say. If your child seems interested, you could continue: "God created sex to be good, and making a husband and wife want to stay together is a good thing. God did not make sex just to help us have babies but to help us want to stay together. Each time a husband and wife have sex they want to stay together more."

6. If they ask why some mothers and fathers do not stay together, you could say that sex helps us want to stay together, but sometimes other things happen that cause

people to want to separate. Or, if a person uses sex in a way that is not considerate, it can be hurtful instead of helpful.

Parent-Child Activity: Option 2

Use Questions to Open Conversation

We covered several topics as part of the cleansing conversations you can have with your nine to twelve year old children. One of the best ways to get such a conversation started is to ask your children questions about what they are seeing and hearing. This takes the heat off them as you are not asking what they may have done on purpose that they are afraid you would be mad at them for. You can get to those questions later, but the following are questions that feel safer for children when you start conversations about sex.

Instructions:

Plan ahead and select a time when your child will not be distracted to have this discussion. It is okay to tell them you are setting aside a time to talk, or you can make it seem spontaneous. When the day and time arrive, look through the following and select **one question** to ask your child.

- I know kids your age look at pornography. Do you ever overhear kids talking about pornography?
- When I was your age, kids told each other jokes about sex. Do you ever hear kids telling jokes like that?
- Do you ever hear kids talking about sexual things?

If they answer "yes," to any of the above, you should ask:
- What kinds of things do they say?
- What do you think about what they are saying?
- What do you think about (whatever the topic was)?
- Do you have any questions for me about this?
- What do you think God would have us do?
- Why do you think God would have us do this?

NOTE: This should not be a conversation that you are trying to drive in any particular direction. The goal is to get your child to start sharing what they are experiencing in their world and thinking through what to do with what they are being exposed to. Let the conversation go where it goes without trying too hard to force it to go where you think it should.

It is always good to share part of your own story if you feel it would be helpful at any point.

8

Preparing a Child for Puberty

Let's be honest, it can be awkward to talk about puberty, for parents and children alike. I was very self-conscious going through puberty as a boy. It started for me at the very beginning of summer after seventh grade. I normally wore tank tops all summer, but I realized it would reveal the new hairs in my armpits, and then *people would know*. For some reason, I felt embarrassed for adults to know that I had entered puberty, so I wore t-shirts and kept my arms down that summer.

At the same time I had an internal pride to be entering puberty. It was exciting to watch my body change and develop. The result of these opposing feelings left me confused and feeling awkward, with absolutely no one I could talk to about what was happening to me.

Parents can feel embarrassed as well. What are we supposed to say to our kids when we notice what is happening to them? It can seem like our kids could not possibly be old enough to be sexually maturing. It doesn't help that so few of us had parents who talked to us about puberty. For many of us, this is uncharted territory.

But this was never intended to be uncharted territory. God created families to be a place where we can discuss absolutely anything. Family is supposed to be our children's safe place.

An Example of What Could Be

A mother shared her story with me. She was a teacher who taught at the same school her boys attended. One day between classes her twelve-year-old son ran excitedly into her classroom, which still had other kids in it, to show his mom two new hairs that had just appeared in his previously bald armpit. His words were, "Look Mom, I got two hairs!"

This is more like what should be happening in our families, but it won't happen if we don't talk about puberty openly with our kids.

What Our Children Need to Know

It is only fair for children to know what is going to happen to them in advance. We don't want them to worry that something is wrong with them when changes comes.

We typically think of teaching children about the physical changes that come with puberty. This is very important, but because that topic has been so well covered by other authors, I will refer you to Appendix B if you want a book to help you with those conversations. There is a section on *The Body & Development* with several resources to help you talk about puberty with your children. Some resources include discussion about emotional changes during puberty as well.

On the other hand, some of you may feel confident in this area and not need extra help to have such a conversation with your child. If you feel ready to explain to your children the physical changes they will experience during puberty, you should feel free do to so.

There are other changes that parenting resources often do not address, or if they address them, they do not align with God's design for sex. In this chapter we will discuss how to teach your children about the changes in the following areas and what these changes do to them. We will discus how changes in:

1. **Sex Hormones** affect emotions & sexual feelings.
2. **Body Growth** affect sleep, diet, & willpower.
3. **Limbic System** affect emotions, novelty, & sexuality.
4. **Pre-Frontal Cortex** affect decision making & willpower.

At this point some of you may be having unpleasant flashbacks of your high-school science class. I was a science teacher for nine years, so that is a rational fear in this case. However, I promise to restrain myself and try to keep this simple. I will use correct scientific terms rather than simplified ideas and this is on purpose. Older children can feel talked down to if we use over-simplified terms too often. Near-pubescent children are sophisticated enough to understand and use the words, "limbic system."

When to Start the Conversation

Ideally, we will start talking about puberty before our children enter puberty, not after. We can guess when our children will go through puberty from our own experience. Whatever age a parent went through puberty is likely similar to the age their same-gender child will. This is certainly not exact, but is an approximate guideline to go by.

We want to give this information before puberty, so you might consider starting these conversations about a year before you expect your child to enter puberty. That gives you lots of time to work these topics in before these changes start to actually happen. You don't have to have all these conversations all at once. This is not a race.

The Effects of Sex Hormones

Testosterone and estrogen are only two of many hormones involved in puberty. It would be unwise to try to teach an eleven-year-old about the complex inner-workings of all the chemicals involved in developing their sexuality. That is a college level class. Instead, we can simply teach them that there are chemicals that their body begins to produce before puberty that cause many changes in their bodies. The physical changes are only some of what is happening inside them.

It is important for parents to understand that the amount of chemical change going on inside our children is enormous. Let's look at just one example—testosterone level change in boys. Boys and girls have testosterone in their system from birth, but during the first two years of puberty in boys testosterone levels increase between 1,500%[47] and 4,900%[48]. That is a tidal wave of hormones!

It is important for us to understand as parents that the forces behind the changes in our children are overwhelming. Our children go from feeling no effect of sex hormones to feeling their full force in a very short period of time. It is somewhat like a child sitting in a car, relaxing obliviously into their seat, then having the car unexpectedly accelerate from zero to 200 miles an hour in 60 seconds. This is going to happen whether any of us like it or not. Let's make sure they have a seatbelt on.

The Effects of Hormones on Emotions

Our children deserve to know that sex hormones cause emotions to feel elevated. The flood of chemicals that causes puberty also causes emotional reactions to be extreme for a while. When a newly pubescent child experiences sadness, they may feel like the world is ending. When they are happy, they may bounce off the walls—more than usual. The same event that would have created a small emotion before may now create a huge emotional response.

I remember explaining this to my daughter before she reached puberty. She rolled her eyes and said she would never act that way. Admittedly, she did react better than I expected, but she also experienced times when she had difficulty dealing with unusually strong feelings. The knowledge we prepared her with before puberty did seem to help her navigate the extreme emotions more effectively. And when she didn't control her emotions, she understood why she couldn't. That knowledge itself was reassuring.

We also need to tell our children that elevated emotional responses serve a purpose God designed for this time in their life. A lot of literature and school curriculum teaches children that the emotional effects of puberty are something annoying they must endure. The reality is that God designed this phase of life for a very specific and good purpose, which we will explore later in this

---

[47] Degroot, Leslie, *Endocrinology*, 4th Edition, W.B. Saunders Company, New York, 2001

[48] J Clin, *Endocrinal Metab*, 1973(6):1132-1142

chapter. God doesn't do anything without a purpose—even allowing elevated emotions during puberty.

When We See Exaggerated Emotions

We will eventually see these very strong emotional reactions once our children enter puberty. When this happens, we can gently point out that what they are experiencing is what we told them about before puberty. We can tell our stories of when we were emotional at their age. This may not be enormously reassuring to a child in the middle of experiencing wild emotions, but it helps a little.

In addition to exaggerated emotions during adolescence, there are the normal mood swings that come with puberty. Ann Martin talks about how she dealt with this with her children:

With my girls, sometimes I thought we are doing okay, and then suddenly one would let out a huge angry outburst. When I saw this kind of thing happen I would remind them that this is normal at their age, which typically calmed them down. With girls and their menstrual cycle, we can help them find a pattern. I try to help my daughters count the weeks and put it on the calendar as a tool to gauge what's going on with them. I do tell them that this is going to be a hard time. My youngest has described it saying, "I'm just kinda grouchy." I tell her it's okay to be grouchy, but it's not okay to be grouchy at me.

I'm not an advocate of girls saying, "Oh, I'm on my period so that's why I'm acting this way." I tell them, "Well, you are, but you have to figure out how to handle it." I teach them that these emotions are going to happen, so we need to learn to deal with them appropriately. I sometimes pull out the emotional charts we used before to help them figure out why they feel mad. They point and say, "Yeah, I'm feeling this way," or "This emotion feels heightened."

I think boys have their own emotional cycles during puberty as well. It may not be as pronounced in boys, but I notice boys having days where they are more emotionally touchy

*than normal for no apparent reason. When we see this
happening, we can help them by asking, "If you're feeling
this way, what do you think is going on?"* [49]

Teenagers sometimes want time alone when they are feeling a
lot of emotions. It is okay for them to go to their room and be alone
to sort out their feelings, but then they need to come out and engage
with the family again.

Emotional Changes and Relationships

It is fair to warn children that relationships with friends may be
more difficult for a while after puberty arrives, as a result of these
heightened emotions. Since their friends are likely going through
puberty around the same time, what they end up with is a bunch of
very emotional and easily offended kids trying to get along. This
partially explains why middle school-aged kids can be so mean to
each other. We can help our children know not to take what their
friends say too personally because they aren't in very good control of
their emotions either.

Tell your children you'll be there to talk through it with them
when their friends act irrationally. Share examples of times when
your friends acted meanly or rudely when you were that age, and
what might have been behind those reactions. It will be reassuring
to your child that you have been through what they are going
through with their friends.

Hormone Effects on Interest in Sex and Romance

We can explain to our children that they will begin to experience
sexual feelings toward others. Some children will desire physical
contact and have a new interest in romance. Most children will
experience a new or elevated desire to see nudity. Children will
begin to experience sexual arousal whether they want to or not,
although they may not know what to call this new sensation. Both
genders can experience any or all of these. This is not a boy or girl
issue, but an adolescent issue.

---

[49] Ibid

Because of the hypersexual culture we live in, many children become interested in nudity and sex before puberty. Even when this is the case, the addition of hormones dramatically increases a child's interest in romance and sex at puberty. There will be a change no matter where the child was at before puberty.

The good news is if we have already been talking about emotions and sexuality, our children will be more comfortable asking for help when they don't know how to handle the feelings inside them. One mother shares a story of how this looked in her family. They had been talking with their son about sexuality starting at age eight. She recounts for us a time when he was older, and she noticed he was reacting strongly to girls and didn't know how to deal with it:

Last summer we were at the beach. I could see it all over his face as our family was setting up our umbrellas and putting out our chairs. It was like he had walked out into a minefield. It was like I could see the bombs exploding all around him. A few minutes later, he came to me and asked me why all the girls were wearing bikinis.

I asked, "Is it hard for you to be here?"

"Yes," he replied.

So I pulled my husband aside and asked him to take our son for a walk. I asked him to share with our son his strategies for coping with the beach bombs. And he did. And he continues to do that, as the need arises.

We can assist our children in situations like this by helping them understand that these romantic and sexual feelings are not only normal, but were specifically designed by God. The message to our children is—these new feelings are actually good, and they have a purpose. We will also need to help them know how to appropriately deal with the new feelings inside them.

Ann Martin shares how one of her daughters brought up the feelings she was having:

My youngest came up to me and said, "Mom, it's really weird; I just want to hug a boy when I'm on my cycle." So that started us talking about her new romantic feelings. I was glad she could bring it up so easily. I told her that this is how our hormones work and how God designed us.[50]

Our children deserve to know that both their new emotions and sexual desires can feel stronger than their ability to make logical choices for a few years. We will explain how this works, and ways you can help them, in the following sections. Prepubescent children need to be made aware that this will be true, but that you will be there to help them through the effects of hormones and that it will be okay.

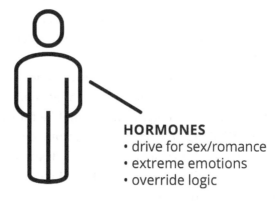

HORMONES
• drive for sex/romance
• extreme emotions
• override logic

The preceding image illustrates a simple three-point summary of the effects of hormones, for which we can prepare our children.

The Effects of Body Growth

Children often go through a growth spurt sometime between the onset of puberty and the end of their teen years. Some children's bodies grow at an alarming rate during this age. When a child's body is growing, it uses up every ounce of energy reserve they have to spare, and sometimes more. Growth takes energy and rapid growth takes a huge amount of energy. That energy has to come from somewhere.

---

[50] Ibid

Puberty and Willpower

Willpower and self-control are not the same thing. Willpower is not just an expression but also a kind of energy. Willpower is what we use in order to practice self-control. Willpower is the energy available to us to do all the things we need to do, from physical activity to making decisions. Our brains use exactly the same kind of energy as our muscles do, and it all comes from the same place. Willpower is essentially a measure of our available blood sugar and rest.[51]

You might think of humans as having a willpower tank, much in the way a car has a gas tank. In the morning, once we are completely awake and have eaten, our willpower tank will be as full as it's going to get that day. We have lots of energy available, including energy to make good decisions.

As the day goes on, we run lower and lower on energy, particularly between meals. Anything at all that we do uses up this reserve of energy, which cannot be fully recharged until we sleep. Walking, having a conversation, and remembering to turn off a light when we leave a room all drain our daily supply. Our brains literally run low on sufficient energy to make good decisions as the day progresses.

In other words, our bodies have a full tank of willpower in the morning and run almost dry by evening, causing us to seek out rest or collapse from exhaustion. Rather than attempt to fight against how we were made, it is wiser to accept that this is part of what it is to be human.

The more difficult a decision is to make—like resisting a cookie when we're on a diet—the more willpower it takes for our brain to make that decision. When we are low on willpower, it feels much harder to resist something we want because we have less energy to resist it.

For example, if there is a plate of cookies near where we are working, it is easy to resist in the morning. It gets harder to resist as

---

[51] Roy F. Baumeister and John Tierney, *Willpower: Rediscovering the Greatest Human Strength* (New York: Penguin, 2011), 43–51.

we walk by at lunchtime. We struggle to control ourselves when we pass the cookie at 3:00, but at 5:00 when we walk by, we find ourselves eating the cookie. The former three times we resisted the cookie partially used up our ability to resist it. By 5:00 there was not enough willpower left to help us resist the cookie.

Our kids are no different. They have less willpower to resist temptation the longer the day progresses. This is a very important thing for them to know as it can help them make choices that help them avoid having to use up their willpower resisting things, like pornography.

Willpower and Body Growth

Everything we've said so far is true for all of us, no matter what age we are. However, adolescent children have an additional component to this puzzle to consider. When an adolescent begins to grow, that growth draws heavily from the same willpower tank that they use to make decisions, including decisions to resist something they want. When an adolescent grows very fast this can nearly empty their willpower tank before they even start the day, leaving them with very little energy to make good decisions.

Body Growth and Resisting Temptation

As you would imagine, adolescents who are growing will find it unusually difficult to resist things they are attracted to, even if they firmly believe these things are bad for them and have vowed not to do them. If it is attractive to them, say pornography, they will find themselves frequently without enough willpower to make the decision they promised themselves they would make to resist it.

Body Growth and Sleep

Because their bodies are growing, teenagers actually need more sleep in order to recharge their willpower tank. The average teenager requires 10 hours of sleep to recharge[52]. That would not be such a problem if it were not true that they also don't fall asleep early very easily.

---

[52] Susan Kim, MD & Kathleen Romito, MD & John Pope, MD, "Teenage Sleep Patterns," *Healthwise*, University of Michigan, March 2018

Teenager's biological clocks change during puberty. Adolescents and teens typically fall asleep later at night and their bodies want to sleep until later in the day.[53] This is a biologically triggered phenomenon, not just an excuse your teenager came up with to stay up late. No, they did not pay me to write that.

Unfortunately, our school schedules start early in the morning, not allowing teenagers to sleep in as their bodies were designed to do. As a result, teenagers typically stay up late but have to get up early. Instead of nine or ten hours of sleep they get six or seven. As a result their willpower tank is never filled up and they run low on energy early in the day.

Body Growth and Food

Every parent knows that adolescents often eat as if they had a hollow leg. This is their body trying to get enough energy to grow and think and perhaps have enough left to learn something at school. Carbohydrates have the most readily available energy so teens often gravitate toward high-carb foods. This is also a biologically driven craving. However, our biology was not designed to take into consideration processed foods and ultra-high carb foods that are everywhere today. Excessive carbohydrate intake causes an initial spike in blood sugar level but soon after results in an energy crash.

The Results of Low Willpower

Body growth, not enough sleep, and poor nutrition all feed into lowering willpower. When an adolescent's willpower is low they have no energy to control emotions or to think rationally. As a result, low willpower makes teenagers irritable, irrational, and act impulsively.[54] When adolescent children are low on willpower, they often give in to whatever is easiest to do because they are too drained to think about consequences. During times when their willpower is low, teens have a greatly diminished ability to resist things that are appealing to them. That includes harmful things like

---

[53] Ibid

[54] Baumeister and Tierney, *Willpower*, 35–49

pornography and sexual fantasy, but also positive things like adventure and becoming interested in the opposite sex.

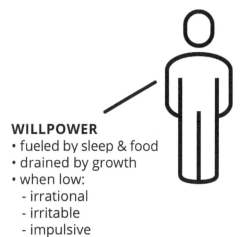

WILLPOWER
• fueled by sleep & food
• drained by growth
• when low:
  - irrational
  - irritable
  - impulsive

The Effects of Limbic System Changes

The limbic system is at the core of the brain. This is the part of the brain that is attracted to new situations and risk, and which drives us to seek out rewards.[55]

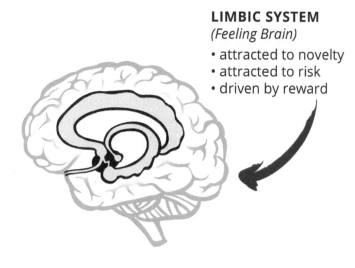

LIMBIC SYSTEM
(Feeling Brain)
• attracted to novelty
• attracted to risk
• driven by reward

---

[55] Jay N. Giedd, The Amazing Teen Brain," *Scientific American,* (June 2015) 36.

Some people refer to this as the "Feeling Brain" because this is where many of our feelings come from. You can decide which term you will use when teaching your child or you may choose to teach both.

The limbic system is the thrill-seeking part of our brain. It does not think rationally or morally. This part of the brain begins to grow around age ten and develops quite rapidly, coming to full maturation around age fifteen.

The more developed our limbic system or feeling brain is, the more an adolescent wants to experience novel and even risky situations. It makes them crave rewards of all kinds, including sexual release. None of these things are bad—in fact, all are necessary for adults. With no limbic system, we would cower from difficult challenges and never have the courage to court a potential spouse. Both adults and teens need not feel ashamed of the drives our limbic system gives us. These are adult desires that God designed for our good.

The Effects of Pre-Frontal Cortex Changes

The pre-frontal cortex is the front portion of our brains. This is where rational thought and decision making occurs. This is the part of our brain that helps us think ahead to imagine the consequences an action might produce. This is also the part of the brain responsible for helping us regulate our emotional responses.

For example, when someone says something a little rude to us, this is the part of our brain that helps us not yell at them but to just let it go and realize it is not really that important. Some people refer to this as our "Thinking Brain." You may choose either or both terms to teach to your children as they near puberty.

Around age ten, a child's prefrontal cortex begins to develop to maturity. This is the same time our feeling brain or limbic system begins to develop. Before age ten children have only a limited ability to think rationally.

PRE-FRONTAL CORTEX
(Thinking Brain)
• forethought
• regulating emotions
• decision making

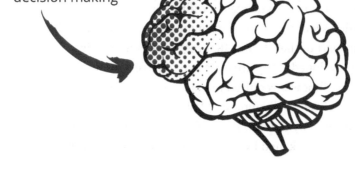

Unlike the limbic system, the prefrontal cortex is not completely developed until sometime in the mid-twenties.[56] That gives at least a ten-year period, mostly in the teen years, when the ability to regulate emotions and think ahead are not completely developed. The feeling brain develops much faster than the thinking brain. During this time adolescents and young adults experience the largest difference between impulse control and judgment. Their drive for novelty, risk, and reward are much higher than their ability to control impulses and make rational decisions. This difference peaks around age fifteen and slowly improves until roughly age twenty-five.[57]

---

[56] Ibid

[57] Ibid

The Four Changes Combined

Let's look now at how all changes in these four areas affect the ability of teenagers to make decisions. We will replace body growth with willpower since the primary result of body growth that we are concerned with are changes in willpower.

Adolescents have extreme emotions due to elevated hormones, but the part of their brains that regulates emotions is underdeveloped. They are attracted to novelty and risk but often lack the willpower required to make rational decisions and resist impulses. The small amount of logic they may possess is easily overpowered by the new flood of hormones running through their bodies and weakened by low willpower to stop and think clearly.

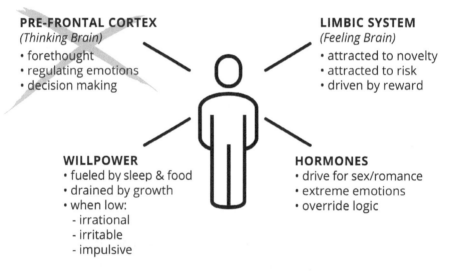

PRE-FRONTAL CORTEX
(Thinking Brain)
• forethought
• regulating emotions
• decision making

LIMBIC SYSTEM
(Feeling Brain)
• attracted to novelty
• attracted to risk
• driven by reward

WILLPOWER
• fueled by sleep & food
• drained by growth
• when low:
  - irrational
  - irritable
  - impulsive

HORMONES
• drive for sex/romance
• extreme emotions
• override logic

What does this mean? For one thing, when we ask our teenagers, "Why did you do that?" and they respond by saying, "I don't know," they are not lying. Teenagers can be as surprised as their parents why they did something thoughtless. They really don't understand why they would have given in to something they should have known was not a good idea. At the time they did whatever they did, their prefrontal cortex or thinking brain was simply not up to the task of reining them in.

Why Would God Do This?

When I was in high school, my school taught that teenagers go through a phase where the brain is not in balance. We were essentially told that we were in a temporary state of being defective. It did not help that, from time to time, the way we acted seemed to support that idea. Nonetheless, this is an unhelpful and inaccurate message to give an adolescent.

God is the one behind our design, and He does not make mistakes. There is a purpose for this decade-long mental alteration we all go through. Our children deserve to know the "why" behind what is happening to them. It helps in our parenting attempts when we understand as well.

When adolescents invite the Holy Spirit to affect them and embrace Jesus' command to love others more than themselves, these apparent flaws turn into enormous strengths. During this ten-year time span in such an adolescent's life the following characteristics are typically true:

1. Extreme emotions make adolescents capable of **extreme compassion** for others. Their heightened emotions make compassion feel stronger and more likely to be expressed.
2. When teenagers feel an **impulse to do good** and help others, it can override logical excuses for not following through. Impulse control is lower during the teen years, and that is supposed to be a good thing. If the impulse is to do something selfless for someone else, it can be good that they tend to act before they think of all the reasons why their efforts might not work.
3. Adolescents are capable of taking great **risks to be vulnerable** with others. Elevated hormones and emotional drives, combined with lower willpower and reason, lead to risk-taking. Being emotionally vulnerable to others can be pretty scary but also very powerful when we are trying to help someone else. Adolescents have a natural ability to do this that is greater than the average adult, because they do not consider the emotional risk.

4. Teenagers **don't think ahead** to consider any negative consequences of giving fully of themselves. Teenagers can more easily put aside worry about all the things that could go wrong in giving of themselves to help someone else. This is a natural byproduct of how their minds work.

5. Teenagers become very **attracted to the opposite sex**, which is necessary to eventually draw them away from their parents to eventually bond in marriage. Sometimes it can be worrisome when we see our adolescents become interested in romance, but this does need to happen if they ever hope to get married. This is the time in their lives that their bodies were designed to become interested in the opposite sex. This is supposed to happen, and it is a good thing.

Changes at Puberty and Sexual Wholeness

Of course, any strength brings with it a weakness. When we are aware of a weakness, we should find others to help us in that area. The Bible is full of stories that illustrate this. David was a passionate man—sometimes too passionate. Nathan was his advisor, who called him back to God when David let his sexual passions get out of control. Samson had great physical strength but great weakness when it came to controlling his sexual urges. Unfortunately, Samson did not allow anyone to act as his mentor or partner, and his weakness eventually destroyed him.

Our teenagers have weaknesses in decision-making that accompany their strengths. God intends for parents to be their mentors, to help them avoid the pitfalls of their weaknesses.

An Adolescent's Weakness

When it comes to pursing sexual wholeness, the unique way teens think creates a serious dilemma for them. Sexual release, or even simply dwelling on sexual or romantic feelings, creates an enormous emotional and physically pleasurable reward. Since teens are driven by reward, are impulsive, and have a diminished ability to foresee negative consequences, it can be extremely difficult for them to deal with sexual impulses in a mature way. This is true even when they are completely convinced that pursuing their sexual impulses would be harmful to them.

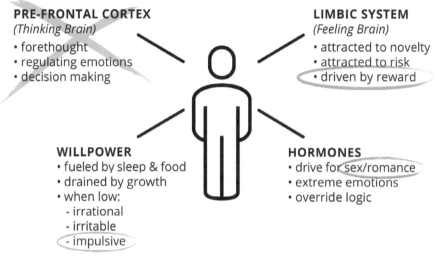

PRE-FRONTAL CORTEX
(Thinking Brain)
• forethought
• regulating emotions
• decision making

LIMBIC SYSTEM
(Feeling Brain)
• attracted to novelty
• attracted to risk
• driven by reward

WILLPOWER
• fueled by sleep & food
• drained by growth
• when low:
 - irrational
 - irritable
 - impulsive

HORMONES
• drive for sex/romance
• extreme emotions
• override logic

Neither the hypersexual culture our teens are surrounded by nor how their brain function is his or her fault. Any weakness to resist temptation is brought on by what are otherwise strengths. We need to stand beside them and help them through this, not condemn them for their feelings or apparent weaknesses.

Our children will not escape these temptations just because they were raised in a godly home and attend church. God knows this, and directs parents to guide them through their developing sexuality as safely as is possible. They will not be perfect but neither has any teenager in the history of the world navigated adolescent sexuality perfectly. Sexual wholeness is something they journey toward, not achieve by age thirteen.

Parental Compensation

As our children's guardians, it is our job to help them think through their choices until they are old enough to do so more reliably themselves. This is not to say that all adolescents make bad choices, or that the ones who do make bad choices all the time. It is simply that adolescents have a very strong tendency to act before they think. This is why we don't let fifteen-year-olds go out and live on their own.

What About God?

Christian parents are unwise to assume that their child's faith will spare them from unwise decisions in their sexuality all the time. An adolescent's commitment to anything is very sporadic and only becomes consistent with maturity, usually after age twenty-five. It is unfair to expect a teenager to be more mature in their spirituality than their sexuality. Both are maturing at the same time in an adolescent and are closely connected. During this time when they are deciding how much they can trust God and His advice, we are responsible for helping them through sexual development. The Bible tells us to mentor our children for a reason.

Ways Parents Can Help

We should talk with our teens about making good decisions, but have compassion to understand that many are at a huge disadvantage in their ability to follow through with rational thought all the time. In addition to conversations you have about sexuality, try some of these things to help compensate for your adolescent's decision-making patterns:

1. Teach everything in this chapter to your children by the time they are fourteen. They deserve to understand what is happening to them.
2. Tell your stories as you feel they are appropriate. This can include unwise decisions you made as a teenager. This helps them believe you understand what they are going through. Remember not to share damaging details or things you have not told your spouse. Watch your teen's reactions to gauge if you are sharing too much.
3. Be supportive, not condescending when they do irrational things.
4. Try to help them eat well. Specifically, ensure they have protein every day, and reduce carbohydrates and sugar consumption. This will help willpower levels remain more consistent with fewer dips during the day.

5. Try to help them get more sleep, aiming for nine hours each night. They won't like it, but we can try to get them to sleep more. You may be limited by school schedules and you may not be able to do this often, but it is worth trying to help them get more sleep.

6. No bedroom or bathroom Internet access. They do not have the restraint to not look at inappropriate material in private places like this.

7. Sets good example by leaving your phone on the table when you use the bathroom. In order to be fair, keep your computer out of your bedroom, too. Don't expect your teenagers to do things you won't do.

8. Don't have discussions about hard or emotional things in the evening, when willpower is low and tempers can flair easily. Make evenings after 6:00 pm as much a conflict-free time as possible.

9. Work with each child to discover times and situations when they are most likely to give in to temptation. Discover ways to have extra safeguards during those times and situations.

10. Ensure that there is frequent parent-child sharing, and accountability where emotions and temptations are discussed openly and without shame.

11. Don't parent alone. Find parents to talk with, about how this is going with your children so you can ask questions and share ideas.

Parent-Child Activity: Option 1

Start a Conversation About Puberty

This activity is recommended for children who are approaching puberty or within the first two years of puberty. The goal is not to discuss everything in the preceding chapter but simply start the conversation in the easiest way possible. If you feel your child falls in this range, consider doing the following with them.

Instructions:

1. Arrange a time to talk with your child that is private and comfortable.
2. Ask your child, "What do you know about the changes that happen with puberty besides changes to your body?"
3. If they mention something about emotions, ask them to clarify what exactly changes related to emotions.
4. Explain to them if they do not know that the same chemicals that cause their bodies to change also cause their emotional reactions to become stronger. Clarify with this fictional example:

A (boy/girl) is eight years old and is told they can't go to a party. They feel disappointed and cry but the next day they forget what happened. At age fifteen the kid's parents use exactly the same words to explain they cannot go to a party they want to attend. This time the teenager yells at their parents, storms out of the room and slams their door. They stay mad at their parents and hardly talk to them for a week. Exactly the same thing happened but the feelings of disappointment and being left out were many times more powerful when the boy/girl was fifteen year old. This is what it looks like to have more powerful feelings after puberty. This fades through the teenage years and emotions return to normal again.

5. Tell a story of when you reacted with extreme emotions as a teenager.
6. If your child has reached puberty, ask them if they have experienced this yet.

7. Talk about ways the two of you can get through times when they experience extreme emotions.
8. Assure them you love them even if this happens.

Parent-Child Activity: Option 2

Explain Changes in the Brain

The extent your child may be interested in what is or will happen in their brain during puberty is something only you can guess at. If you think they are ready and potentially interested, use this page to teach your child what happens to the human brain between ages ten and twenty five.

PRE-FRONTAL CORTEX
(Thinking Brain)
• forethought
• regulating emotions
• decision making

LIMBIC SYSTEM
(Feeling Brain)
• attracted to novelty
• attracted to risk
• driven by reward

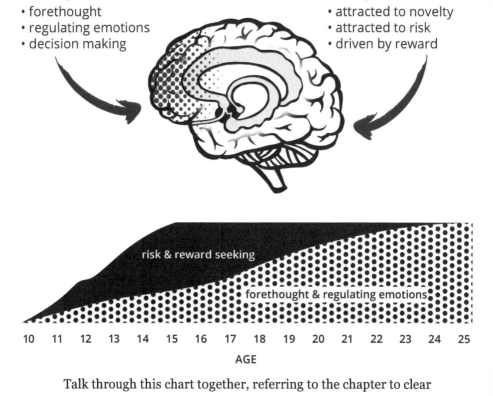

Talk through this chart together, referring to the chapter to clear up any misunderstandings. Once you have done that, discuss the following questions together.

1. What does God have to do with all of this?
2. How could this 10-year period of change in how we think be used for good?

3. How might this make it more difficult to resist things like pornography during the teen years?
4. What are some ways you can work together to reduce the chances of making poor decisions about things like sex and pornography while this is happening?

Parent-Child Activity: Option 3

Teach Your Child About Willpower

This activity could be done with any child old enough to be interested. Read the following to your child and discuss the answers together.

Not many people use the word "willpower" correctly. Scientists use willpower to mean the amount of energy inside your body that is available to be used. Each of our bodies is able to carry a certain amount of willpower and no more. We don't really have a willpower "tank" like the picture below, but this is an easy way to understand how it works.

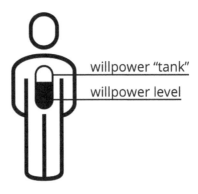

willpower "tank"
willpower level

Everything we do or think requires willpower or energy and everything we do or think uses up a little willpower. Here are a few things that need willpower to do and use it up when they happen:

- Opening your eyes
- Walking, running, climbing, or jumping
- Talking to your friend
- Deciding what to say
- Doing math
- Not reacting to someone who is being really annoying
- Growing taller

The harder it feels like a particular thing is to do, the more willpower it takes to do it. Feeling "hard to do" means you have to use a lot of willpower to do it. This includes trying to figure out schoolwork or making a choice between two things you really want.

This means every time you do or think anything, your willpower "tank" gets emptier. When your willpower tank is near empty, it becomes really hard to do anything, even thinking. We can tell when our willpower is getting low because we feel tired.

Willpower comes from food and sleep. We fill our tank back up by eating and sleeping. When we wake up and eat breakfast, our willpower tank is as full as it's going to get that day. If we didn't get enough sleep, that means we start with a tank that is not very full.

As the day goes on, we do eat some, but this only partially refills our tank. By the end of the day, we have very little willpower left, and it becomes hard to do or think as well as we can earlier in the day. This is what happens when you can't figure out how to do homework at night that you know should not be hard to figure out.

Questions to Discuss Together:
1. List five physical things and five thinking things that will be harder to do with a low willpower tank.
2. What are some ways a person might get into trouble during times they have low willpower?
3. A boy or girl is thirteen and starts to grow really fast, growing four inches in one year. Thinking about willpower, what would this do to him or her during that year?
4. A kid has decided they do not want to look at pornography because they know it is harmful. Can you describe a situation where this same kid finds it harder than normal to resist looking at pornography because of willpower?
5. We know that our willpower is usually lowest in the evenings. What are some things you and your family could put in place in the evenings so that you do not need as much willpower to make good decisions?
6. Each of you share a story of a time you think you had low willpower and how that turned out.

9

Addressing Masturbation

I do not want any reader to think that the fact I am devoting an entire chapter to this one subject that masturbation is somehow more important or a bigger issue than others within an adolescent's sexuality. It is not. Masturbation is not the most important issue a teenager faces.

I put aside space for this topic because this is the topic I am asked the most questions about. This is also the topic that many parents have the most fear in knowing how to discuss. This is no ones fault. Very few of us had a parent who talked to us about masturbation, other than perhaps to say, "it's normal, don't worry about it," or "its bad so don't do it."

My only goal in this chapter is to help you feel more comfortable talking about masturbation so that you can talk about it with your adolescent child. I will start by giving you information to improve your comfort level. Then I will offer some conversation tips for discussing masturbation with your adolescent child.

Like every other subject, we will talk about masturbation openly and honestly. It doesn't help our children or us if we ignore this.

What Parents Should Know

Not all Self-Touching is Masturbation

Boys and girls of any age may touch their own genitals. Young children may touch their genitals out of curiosity. They may do it again if it feels good. In these cases, they have no concept of sex or sexuality, this is just a physical sensation they discovered. This behavior is no different than a young child picking their nose[58]. This is not considered masturbation.

If a parent discovers a child self-touching, the number one thing we must do is not overreact. Reacting with panic, anger, or extreme embarrassment can cause a child to feel shame about their body and sexuality. Shame is the primary driver in addictions and the last thing we want our child to associate with any part of their sexuality. If a parent is concerned about the behavior, young children are typically easy to redirect by showing affection or helping them find something else to do. There is usually no need to point out the behavior or say it is "bad."

Curiosity

Initial experiences with masturbation in adolescents are typically due to curiosity about their own body or accidentally achieving orgasm due to naiveté. An adolescent exploring the new body God gave them is an innocent act. Yes, that might lead to masturbation but not necessarily. New adolescents are curious about their own changing bodies, as were we at their age.

Body Changes

We have been teaching our children that sex is God's idea and is good. We have been teaching our children that their sexual organs are not to be ashamed of and were designed by God to be specially honored. Before puberty, we told them of the changes that were coming to their bodies and that God designed all these changes to occur. Many adolescents find it difficult to believe that they will have

---

[58] Ann Byle, What to do When Young Kids Masturbate, *Focus on the Family*, (2015) Retrieved from: focusonthefamily.com/parenting/sexuality

the kinds of feelings their parents are talking about. It all can seem a little gross to them, which is normal.

Then the changes come and many adolescents are completely shocked at how their new bodies react. Simply lying down on a bed at night can cause an adolescent boy to become physically aroused and send sensations through him he has no idea how to control. Putting on a bra can cause an adolescent girl's breasts to become stimulated and physically arouse her when she had no idea that could even happen. Taking a shower can unexpectedly turn into an erotic feeling event to any adolescent. None of this is their fault. Their hormone levels are off the chart and their bodies are reacting exactly how they were designed to react.

Does any of this sound familiar? None of this is masturbation, but it is easy to see how even innocent activity could lead to masturbation in adolescence. When these intense feelings are so new, adolescents simply don't know what to do with them. Early masturbation experiences often have nothing to do with sexual fantasy or pornography and can happen by accident or out of innocent actions, causing unexpected results.

Being Honest About Masturbation

Masturbation is going to happen. Virtually all boys[59] and nearly half of teen girls[60] are going to masturbate. Nothing you as a parent can do will stop that. This book is about being honest, so let's not ignore what really happens in adolescence with masturbation. The question is what do we do with this information? Fortunately, there really are ways we can help, but first we need to better understand what is behind masturbation.

The Real Problem

Masturbation in teens is typically not about sex but a way to feel better. Masturbation may begin out of curiosity, but in most cases it quickly becomes a means of escaping uncomfortable emotions and

---

[59] Dr. Archibald Hart, "The Sexual Man", (1994) 119

[60] J.D. Atwood & J. Gagnon, *Journal of Sex Education and Therapy*, 13:2, (1987):35-42

disappointment. Teenagers may not be aware of this, but that does not make it less true.

You may recall the following chart that we discussed earlier in chapter six. Older children can inadvertently learn to use sexual stimulation as a means to cover up negative emotions. Masturbation can easily become the "go-to" form of sexual stimulation an adolescent uses to escape from having to think about something embarrassing that happened, a friend who rejected them, or any other form of disappointment. They may be completely unaware that they are doing this, yet if we were to study their behavior, we would find the times they masturbate are usually after some form of emotional discomfort has occurred.

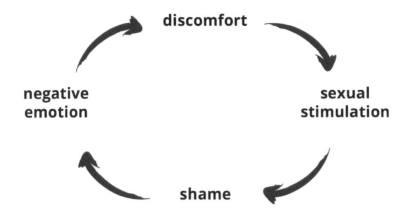

In this sense masturbation is an immature means of dealing with disappointment and stress. The problem is not masturbation; the problem is an inability to deal with unpleasant feelings. The problem is made worse by the fact that their emotions are much more exaggerated at this age and negative feelings feel a lot worse than they used to. A ten-year-old who is able to cope well with negative feelings may find it much more difficult at age fourteen. Masturbation can easily become a way of escape when no better solution is available.

Pornography is a Separate Problem

Masturbation often becomes intertwined with pornography use. We have already discussed how the kind of pornography that exists today is particularly harmful to young minds. When masturbation accompanies pornography use, it intensifies the damage done by pornography. Masturbation while viewing pornography cements an attachment to pornography because that is what sexual release is intended to do: create a bond to what we are looking at during sexual stimulation.

In the case of a teen who is purposefully viewing pornography and masturbating, it is the pornography that we must focus our attention on first. The physical act of masturbation does not cause attention deficit, loss of willpower, social anxiety, decreased satisfaction with real sex, erectile dysfunction in young adult males, negative body image, and increased impulsivity like modern pornography does. Focus on the most dangerous behavior first, which in this case is clearly pornography use.

Once pornography use is eliminated, masturbation becomes much easier to address.

Considerations for Boys

Ejaculation is not a choice for boys. Once puberty arrives, the male body is designed to escalate sexual tension until it overpowers him and his body reaches sexual release. Adolescents have the lowest ability to control this built-in escalation. If a teen boy manages to refrain from masturbation while awake, his body will climax while he is asleep.

Wet dreams impact boys more than we sometimes admit. When an adolescent boy has a dream so erotic that he ejaculates, he will often wake up during that process. If this happens he may remember the erotic dream very vividly. The fact that he did not decide to have that dream in no way diminishes the sexual images now locked in his head.

The Bible does not mention or even allude to masturbation, yet it discusses nocturnal emissions in three places[61] and gives direction as to what to do when this occurs. In short, the scriptures tell men and boys to cleanse themselves from the experience of a wet dream.

---

[61] Leviticus 15:16-32, Leviticus 22:4, Deuteronomy 23:10

The Bible recognizes that a nocturnal emission can affect our minds and we should not simply ignore it.

Compulsive Masturbation is Harmful

When masturbation becomes a compulsive or frequent habit, we can definitely say it is harmful. Here are some ways we know this is not good for our teenagers:

1. It can imprint their sexual attraction on things that are unhelpful to them.
2. It teaches them to be impatient and to expect sex all the time, which will not happen in marriage.
3. It prevents them from learning to deal with emotions.
4. It teaches them that sex is all about them rather than about giving to a spouse.

Compulsive masturbation keeps an adolescent in an immature state of sexual development. They need to "grow up" in their sexuality, leaving masturbation behind, before marriage can ever provide a fulfilling sex life.

Moving Away from Masturbation Takes Time

Moving away from masturbation is a matter of maturity. Maturation of any kind takes time. Masturbation is a childish sexual behavior that can be outgrown. Just as we are patient for our children to mature in other areas, we need to be patient with them as they mature in their sexuality.

Outbursts of anger are another childish behavior we want our children to outgrow.

> *Get rid of all bitterness, rage and anger, brawling and slander, along with every form of malice.*[62]
> *—The Apostle Paul*

Any parent of a teenager can testify that progress in maturing beyond anger outbursts can be quite slow. Anger outbursts are something we consider childish, but we know adults still sometimes have outbursts. Maturing beyond masturbation is not different.

---

[62] Ephesians 4:31 (NIV)

John W Fort

Maturing in sexuality for a teenager means learning to mature their sexuality beyond needing masturbation to feel better. This will take time—and by time I mean a few years—and even then masturbation is still likely to happen every once in a while.

Masturbation is one of many childish behaviors to be outgrown. When we view masturbation in perspective like this, it becomes much easier to talk about with our adolescents.

Things to Avoid as a Parent

An expectation or hope that your child will never masturbate is unhelpful to everyone. Half of all girls will never masturbate and a tiny percentage of boys will not. Most adolescents will masturbate, however, no matter what is done to avoid it. It is more helpful to think of masturbation, if it happens with your adolescent, as something to be outgrown in time.

It is unhelpful to use the words "right" or "wrong" when discussing masturbation with an adolescent. Doing so misses the point our teenagers need to understand. We have already discussed how masturbation can occur somewhat accidentally. After such experiences, continued masturbation is typically a reaction to something. Our focus needs to be on that thing that masturbation is a reaction to. Behavior cannot change until we identify and address the thing a teenager is reacting to.

Never shame a child for masturbating. Shame causes a teen to isolate and withdraw from you and God. That is the opposite of what you want to happen.

What to Say to Your Adolescent

You have a lot of background information now. Let's look at simplified discussion points you might consider having with your child when you think they are old enough. Only use what you feel comfortable saying with your child.

We can Talk About Masturbation

You will hear your friends talk about masturbation and you can bring your questions to your parents. This is no different than any other topic related to sex in that we can talk honestly about it.

Adolescents and Teens Usually Masturbate

If you masturbate, you are not abnormal or bad. Yes, masturbation can lead to problems, but masturbation does not define who you are or define your relationship with God. Talk about it with God and with us if you do masturbate as that will help remove shame.

Wet Dreams Happen to Teen Boys

This happens a lot with some boys and very rarely with others. When you have a wet dream, you may wake up in the middle of it and remember the sexual things going on in your dream. You are not a bad person because you dreamed a sexual dream. If you feel embarrassed or ashamed of what you dreamed, you should absolutely talk to God about it. You can even ask God to "clean your mind" of those images. You can also talk to your dad, as he knows what you just went through and can help.

Masturbation with Pornography or Sexual Fantasy is Harmful

We have already talked about how pornography is harmful. Masturbation while looking at pornography or having a sexual fantasy locks those images into your mind and makes them very hard to forget. This is something we can work together to avoid.

Compulsive Masturbation is Harmful

Masturbating every day or more than once a day sets a bad pattern that will not help you.

1. It can imprint your sexual attraction on things that are unhelpful to you.
2. It teaches you to be impatient and to expect sex all the time, which will not happen in marriage.
3. It prevents you from learning to deal with your emotions.
4. It teaches you that sex is all about you rather than about giving to a spouse.

Masturbation is a Childish Response to Negative Emotions

Once pornography use is under control, you will probably find the main reason you masturbate is to feel better rather than face stress, anxiety, or disappointment. Masturbation does not help but only delays what you need to deal with. Growing up means learning to deal with unpleasant situations and feelings instead of masturbating to avoid them. We usually do this by talking about the feelings you have before they overwhelm you.

Moving Away from Masturbation is a Process

If stopping all at once does not work you can try reducing the frequency of masturbation. You should definitely remove pornography and fantasy from the equation. Reducing the frequency of masturbation does count as a step of maturity.

Talk to God About Masturbation

There is nothing God does not want to talk to you about. God wants you to talk to Him like a real person, not just ask Him for forgiveness and assistance. He wants you to talk to Him about your sexual feelings. You can talk to God about any times you have masturbated. You can ask God to help you find the emotions you may be hiding from when you masturbate. Real conversations like this are the most helpful. Then, if you feel like He is telling you something or giving you advice about masturbation, you should listen to what He says and trust it.

Parent-Child Activity: Option 1

A First Conversation

If your child is about a year away from puberty, or if they have already entered puberty and you've never talked about masturbation, you might consider this exercise. I would recommend the same gender parent as the child have the conversation, although that is not absolutely required.

Instructions:

Make a date with your child and go somewhere private to talk. This could be a car ride if you can't think of anywhere else to go. Then have the following conversation:

1. Say, "I want to talk to you about masturbation. I know this is an embarrassing topic, but we can discuss this like anything else."
2. Tell your child what your parents told you about masturbation, even if it was nothing. Tell them if this was helpful to you.
3. Tell your child questions or confusion you had about masturbation at their age, including what you imagined God thought about it.
4. Ask your child if they have heard other kids talk about masturbation and what they said if so.
5. Ask your child if they have any questions about masturbation. Answer their questions honestly.
6. If your child asks you if you ever masturbated be honest with them. Tell them how you learned about it and how old you were. Do not go into any detail but let them know this is something they can share with you by setting an example of sharing honestly with them.
7. If they volunteer that they have already masturbated you can go to the next exercise.
8. Tell them that you want to be where they learn correct information about sexuality, including masturbation. Tell them you want them to come to you if they ever have any questions at all about masturbation in the future.

9. This is a good place to end the conversation. You do not need to ask if they have masturbated or thought about it. This is just a first conversation.

Parent-Child Activity: Option 2

Responding to Masturbation

This is a conversation to consider having with a child the first time they tell you or you discover that they have engaged in masturbation.

Instructions:

Do not put this conversation off but get somewhere private and talk with them now. This is not a conversation to put on the calendar. Give your full and undivided attention to your child.

1. **Thank them for telling you.** If they told you, they just honored you with what is probably the most personal part of their life to date. Don't treat this like it is a huge deal but show respect for their honesty.

2. **Say, "You are not in trouble."** Whether your adolescent admitted to masturbation or was somehow caught you must assure them before saying anything else that they are not in trouble. Saying "You are not in trouble," removes shame from the equation. Shame will drive our children from God so it needs to be eliminated as soon as possible. You may want to hug your child or tell them you love them. They need to know we do not think less of them for masturbating.

3. **Tell your story.** If you have not done so yet, now is the time to tell your own story of the first time you masturbated. Keep it simple with no details but say how old you were and how you discovered it. Then tell them how you felt later about what you had done. Tell them how you thought God felt about you. Let your adolescent know you have been where they are. You are strengthening your relationship with them, which will make future conversations much easier.

4. **Tell them they are normal.** Make sure they understand that masturbation is something most adolescents do. It is good to explain that this is not God's ultimate plan for sexuality and this is something they will want to mature beyond doing. None-the-less, it is something almost all teens struggle to move beyond.

Parent-Child Activity: Option 3

Helping an Adolescent Mature

Here are some things you can do to help a teen that struggles with masturbation. When they admit to masturbating during a parent-child check-in:

1. **Find out if lust was involved.** Ask if they were looking at pornography or engaging in sexual fantasy. Check their understanding by asking how pornography and sexual fantasy are harmful to them and others. If you notice your child looking ashamed, remind them that we all fall short of our goals sometimes and learning to walk away from lust is a process.

2. **Find out if they were coping.** They may not remember, but ask what had been happening before this event. Were they worried about something? Had someone been unkind to them? If they were experiencing a negative emotion before they masturbated ask them what they could do next time instead to deal with that feeling.

3. **Is there a pattern developing?** Is there a day or time of day when masturbation occurs more often? What else is going on or was going on that may have been a contributing factor? What does this tell us about what might influence your adolescent to engage in masturbation? Is there something we can do to change the situation or the adolescent's response to it?

4. **Tips for bedtime.** If this happened at night, help them come up with ideas that could help them redirect their arousal before going to sleep. Ideas might include:
   - Allow positive music to play softly as they fall asleep
   - Pray and thank God for what they are grateful for
   - Recall fond memories of family or time with friends
   - Have them read a book until they are too sleepy to continue
   - Encourage them to sleep with their door open once they've changed for bedtime

10

Emotional Resilience in Older Children

If we started talking about emotions when our children were young, we can hope that they have acquired some skills by their teen years. Teenagers should be able to clearly identify the feelings they have; beyond the simplified descriptions of "mad, sad, and happy." Teenagers should be able to determine what events or circumstances were the origin of the feelings they are currently experiencing. We may need to help them pause and think for a moment, but they should know how to do this. Finally, teenagers should have begun to practice thinking about the most helpful ways to deal with feelings when they have them.

If you are reading this book for the first time and your children are already teenagers, you may need to catch your teens up on their emotional development in these three areas. You may want to go back to chapters four and six and look through the exercises listed there. You may need to modify them some so that teenagers do not feel like you are treating them as a child since those exercises were designed for younger children. In other words, rather than calling an activity a game, you might say you want to talk to them about their feelings; doing the same basic exercise but using different words to describe it.

Congratulations for Completing Emotions: Level 2!

Level 3 Begins Now

As we discussed in chapter eight, teenagers experience elevated or exaggerated emotions. This means it can be much more difficult for them to manage feelings that they had mastered earlier.

Teenagers can appear to go backward in their ability to react well to emotions. This is not really true. The feelings teenagers experience feel much different than they did before. All the skills they learned when they were younger will help them significantly, but they need to apply those skills to a whole new level of emotions. Put in words a teenager would understand; they just moved up to the next level in the Emotional Development Game and this level is harder. Everything happens faster, but the same skills that got them through the last level will work here. They just have to react faster. Just like moving up a level in a video game.

We will see our teenagers reacting with exaggerated emotions due to the new hormones surging through them and their more developed limbic system. When we see this happen, we can remind them gently, "This is what I was talking about when I said your emotions will feel very strong." We can remind them that it is not their fault, and that we understand what they are going through. It is okay to tell them, "I can see you are upset and that is okay, but the rest of us deserve to not have to tip-toe around you. Let us know what you need from us but allow us to be happy."

Key Emotional Skills for Teens

After puberty emotional feelings and sexual feelings start to get blurred together. This is normal and an example of how our sexuality is intertwined in all aspects of our lives. Even for children who were very good at avoiding things like pornography and sexual fantasy before puberty, it is common for them to suddenly begin to struggle to resist them. Sexuality is more than sex drive, however. Some teens may express romantic feelings as a result of an emotionally charged event that was in no way sexual.

A teenager may understand what event or circumstance caused their feelings; they may be able to clearly identify what emotion they feel, but they may also experience a romantic or sexual feeling and not know what to do with it.

Two Illustrations

Let us say a teenager is complemented by another teen of the opposite gender. They feel happy inside and are able to express that the emotion behind their happiness is feeling accepted and wanted. At the same time, they also feel romantically or sexually aroused. This is new to them and they may not know what to do with this new feeling.

Let us say a teenager discovers they were not invited to a movie that all his or her friends are going to. They feel sad and are able to verbalize that the emotion behind their sadness is feeling rejected or unwanted. When they come home, they also notice they feel either romantically or sexually aroused but may not see any connection between this feeling and being left out.

Coping with New and Stronger Feelings

There are two kinds of sexual feelings in the illustrations above. The first is a normal reaction teens can experience due to the emergence of a more adult sexuality. It is normal for a teenager to feel some romantic or sexual attraction to someone of the opposite gender who is nice to them. In the ideal world, they would feel comfortable enough with their parents to tell them about such experiences. Talking through any feeling, even sexual or romantic, takes some of the edge off. By talking about a feeling, we process it in our minds, making it easier for us to move on to other things rather than obsess about it.

The second example was of a sexual reaction to a negative feeling. This is an indication of a teenager not processing a negative feeling but trying to escape from it through sexual lust of some kind. This is the area we can help our teenagers the most. To do so we will need to help them connect the dots so that they can see how events and circumstances affect sexual feelings. Then we need to help them find healthy ways to deal with those feelings, rather than try to escape them.

Even if a child was good at dealing with emotions before puberty, this is a new level and the feelings are much stronger. They will need our help to come up with strategies to deal with the stronger emotions at this level of the game.

Discuss Feelings Frequently

Pay close attention to your teen's body language, attitude, and behavior. When they display evidence that they are experiencing a feeling that is hard for them, ask them about it. There is no need to keep secret why you are doing this. It is perfectly fine to tell your thirteen-year-old that you want to talk with them about their feelings more often because they will be harder to deal with.

Teens do not like being treated differently than adults, so don't. You tell them about your feelings as often as you ask about theirs. If something annoying happened to you during the day, tell your teen about it, how you felt, and what you did to deal with it. Then ask how their day went. When we do this, we are not treating our teens like children. We are beginning to treat them like adults by having more adult conversations with them. This greatly improves the chances they will willingly share their feelings with us.

You should have these conversations about feelings at least once a week but I would encourage you to do so even more often. It does not have to be a set routine, but it is good to try to check in with every adult and teen in the family daily if possible. This is not more work for you. You already talk to your kids every day; this just changes what you are talking about.

You can also use texting as a way to share feelings. To model this, you might text your teen during the day if something happens that creates a strong feeling in you. Hopefully, they will respond in kind. Simply expressing a feeling to someone who cares about us takes much of the load off. See if you can create a family pattern of expressing feelings regularly rather than bottling them up inside.

Parent-Child Check-ins

By age thirteen, talking about emotions and sexuality begin to blur together. Parents will need to start having regular conversations with teens to help them know what to do with both emotions and sexuality. This is different and in addition to your more frequent sharing of how each of you is feeling. These may be regular meetings you schedule with your child, perhaps once a week, or something you do whenever you see an opportunity to talk, like riding together in the car. You might have a special name for these conversations, such as "accountability" or "man/woman meetings," or you may choose to have no special name. This is entirely up to the personality of your children and what works best for them.

During these conversations, you will be finding out what your child is experiencing both emotionally and in their developing sexuality. At this age, we begin helping them connect the dots between their emotional, spiritual, and sexual selves. There are three elements we want to discuss in these meetings or conversations. Those are 1) the emotions to pay most attention to, 2) what we should do when those emotions happen, and 3) what we are trying to avoid as negative reactions to those emotions. While our focus in these conversations will be mostly on emotions and what to do with them, we start this process by looking at what we are trying to avoid, as that points the way to the other two elements.

What we are Trying to Avoid

We could make lengthy lists of sexual things we do not want our children to engage in. This conversation, however, is not about setting rules for your child to follow. This conversation is about asking our child to decide what they want to avoid. This is their sexuality and none of this will work if it is not their idea.

Research has shown that it does not work to try to stop or refrain from a long list of behaviors. When we try to focus on too many things, we spread our willpower too thin and find we are unable to achieve any of our goals. For this reason, we want to limit the number of things we focus on avoiding with our child. Two or three is plenty.

During these discussions, it is not fair for the child to be asked to talk about unhealthy or immature sexual behaviors they are trying to avoid if we share nothing that is similarly sensitive. This means that we as parents need to tell our child things we are trying to avoid. Adults are no less likely than teenagers to use pornography or engage in sexual fantasy, and it is fair for teenagers to know this. Adults also use things like alcohol, TV, and Social Media to escape negative feelings. If lust is not an issue perhaps one of these might be something a parent would share they want to avoid using as a coping mechanism. All of us have something to work on; be honest about yours.

Remember that when sharing our story we need to be careful to do no harm. We do not want to add an unnecessary burden to our child. Instead we want our children to know they are not alone in their journey. We do not want them to feel a new weight of being responsible for a parent's problems.

As we discussed before, you must have shared past sexual struggles with your spouse before you can share the same thing with your teenager. You should not share any details that might "paint a vivid picture" in your teenager's mind. You should have your own support in place surrounding any current struggles you have before sharing those struggles with your teenager.

Try to put yourself in a teenager's shoes. If you were a teenager, would you rather hear your parent tell you, "I looked at pornography last week," or "I didn't reach my goal of avoiding lust recently so I called my support team Tuesday and am talking with God about that?" Of course, to be able to say the latter a parent struggling with lust would need their own support or accountability network, and may even be seeing a counselor.

We have to set a good example for our children; which includes getting our own help if needed. The reality in this day and age is that most of us should have some form of accountability with other safe adults. Our children are not the only ones constantly exposed to sexual misinformation. As in our children, those images and thoughts need to be washed from our minds through cleansing conversation with safe adults.

After some discussion, each of you should come up with a couple of things you will work on avoiding. Preferably these will be the things each of you is most likely to do, not something you know you won't do. You then agree to share with each other how you are doing on avoiding these things.

However, just trying to avoid something that we feel drawn to does not work. We need two more elements, which is what we get to next.

Determining the Emotions to Watch

You can explain to your older child or teen that things like pornography, fantasy, and masturbation can easily become a way to escape from painful feelings. The things each of you just decided to avoid become a reaction to painful emotions. Not all emotions are painful enough to cause us to want to escape, however. The next step is to help each other discover which emotions are hardest for each of you do deal with. This will take some time.

Some children under age fourteen may have a hard time imagining using pornography, fantasy, or masturbation to escape a negative feeling. They may look at you as if you are speaking a different language. That is okay. You still need to plant this concept in their head as soon as they reach puberty, no matter what age that is.

A newly pubescent child may engage with pornography, fantasy, or masturbation for reasons that have nothing to do with avoiding emotions. In such cases, their behavior is likely a reaction to curiosity and the effect of hormones that they have not yet learned to control. But, in time, most teenagers do begin to use some form of sexual stimulation to escape from negative feelings. In fact, this is what often reveals the emotions we need to pay most attention to.

It is quite likely that each of you will have to fail at avoiding the behaviors you are trying to avoid in order to discover which emotion is the greatest trigger for you. At first, you can only guess at which emotions are painful enough to cause you to violate your decision to avoid something. When you notice a pattern of a particular event or emotion leading one of you to engage in the behavior you wanted to avoid, then you know what needs attention.

Sexual wholeness is a journey, and there are many stumbles along the way. Those stumbles point to what each of us needs to pay more attention to in order to become more sexually whole. Sexual purity is not something a teenager starts with and tries to protect. Sexual purification it is a process of removing contaminants, but we first have to identify the contaminants. A behavior, such as sexual fantasy, is not in itself the contaminant but a symptom that points to the contaminant. The contaminant may be something like experiencing rejection and not knowing what to do with that.

You and your child should each try to guess which emotions would be most painful for you. It is okay if you just guess. We all have to start somewhere.

Finding the Best Reactions to Emotions

Now that each of you has a couple of emotions that you believe are most painful, we can come up with some solutions. This is the exciting part: when we have positive things to do to work toward sexual wholeness. Just focusing on trying to stop doing something is rarely effective. What helps is having something positive to do that takes us away from what we want to avoid. This is the primary focus of our check-ins with our teenagers.

Have a discussion about what each of you might do the next time you experience the painful emotions you came up with. One of you might decide to call or text a specific person to tell them what happened and how you feel. You might decide that going on a walk and talking to God would help. You might choose an activity that you really enjoy rather than sit alone and feel bad.

Each of you tries to come up with two or three ideas and share them with each other. When you have future check-ins, this is the main thing you will ask each other, "Did you do what you said you would do when you felt a negative emotion?"

Putting a Check-in Together

After you have determined what each of you want to do next time you have a painful emotion, you can begin to have check-ins. This might be once a week or whenever an opportune time comes up, like riding in the car. You can make it rather formal or informal. Do what works best for you and your child.

During these conversations, each of you should be divulging times you feel tempted or give in and do something you wanted to avoid. When your child makes such a confession, you can help them analyze what they were feeling just before the temptation came. We can ask questions like:

- What was happening before you felt sexually tempted?
- What emotion were you feeling?
- Were there other times when similar things or feelings happened and you escaped like this?
- Is there a pattern emerging?
- Did you do what you planned on doing when a negative emotions happens?
- Is there something you could do differently next time?

By helping our children talk through feelings that commonly precede temptation, we help them identify the emotions that are most important to care for. You may discover that the emotions you thought were most important are not and that there are others that cause temptation more often. It is usually in this process that our teenagers discover what emotions to pay most attention to and what they can do to resolve them.

An Example

I started having these conversations with my son when he was twelve. He seemed confused by the idea and was never able to connect a negative emotion with times he did one of the things he wanted to avoid. Then, when he was fourteen, something happened that turned the light on for him. Because we talked weekly about how each of us was doing, he began to realize that a pattern was emerging. The one time he struggled with sexual fantasy was walking home from school. This is his story of what he learned:

In conversations my dad and I had about purity, we talked about the times when I was walking home from school and started having problems with temptations. I would be tempted to want to fantasize or think about sexual things.

Then I would come home and wonder what was going on. I didn't know why it was that I had these temptations while walking home from school. I started talking to my dad about it, and he would ask me questions about my walk home. We eventually figured out together that while I was walking home, I felt like I was alone. I'm an extrovert, I love talking, and I love human interaction. The time spent walking home, just thirty minutes, was enough time to make me feel lonely, with no one to talk to. In my mind, I knew that fantasy made me feel better, so I was tempted to turn to that.[63]

This is what we are trying help our children do when we talk to them about their emotions and temptation. We want to help them identify which emotions can make them want to escape into fantasy. When we help our children uncover these emotions, we uncover the situations and emotions they need to address. In this case, feeling lonely was the emotion my son couldn't deal with well. We had never addressed it in the two years we had been doing check-ins because to that point he had never realized this was one of his most painful emotions. The times he gave into sexual fantasy pointed to the problem, and then we knew what to work on.

A Way of Escape

No temptation has overtaken you but such as is common to man; and God is faithful, who will not allow you to be tempted beyond what you are able, but with the temptation **will provide the way of escape** *also, so that you will be able to endure it.*[64]
—*The Apostle Paul*

God tells us that He provides a way of escape when temptation happens. We as parents must help our children understand how this works. Paul's wording in this case is a little confusing because we have been using the word "escape" to mean escaping from an

---

[63] Ibid
[64] 1 Corinthians 10:13, emphasis added

emotion, which is a negative behavior. Perhaps it would be easier if we modified Paul's words like so:

> ...but with the temptation will provide the way **[to resolve your painful emotion]** also, so that you will be able to endure it.

This is entirely within the context of what Paul is saying. For this to help our children they must know what ways of resolving emotions exist; and second, they have to choose to use them.

My son and I worked through this whenever he found a new emotion or situation that caused sexual temptation for him. He discovered that feeling lonely caused him to want to escape into sexual fantasy. This is what happened once he had that information:

> After talking about it some more, we thought that one thing I could do was, while walking home from school, I could call or text my dad. Since he was at work he couldn't always pick up the phone or text back right away. When he answered right away we would talk, but even when he didn't pick up I'd leave him a message. I didn't even say that I was tempted; I would say that I was walking home and ask how he was doing and tell him about my day. That was enough that I knew when we both got home he would talk to me. That helped my temptation to completely go away when I walked home from school.[65]

With a little help, my son found a way of escape when he felt tempted to fantasize on the way home from school. He came to learn that he needed to contact someone when he felt lonely. Then the temptation never came in the first place. What actually happened was he contacted me on his way home from school every day, just as a precaution, for several months. Eventually, he was able to come to God for comfort rather than always need to call someone. It did not take long at all before he no longer felt any temptation to fantasize on his way home from school.

---

[65] Ibid

This is just one example of how check-ins can be a way a parent can help a child move toward sexual wholeness. We can help our children determine which situations and emotions need to be addressed and how to find a way they can resolve the situation rather than allow fantasy or some other sexual behavior to occur.

Emotional Resilience

There are a number of things teenagers go through as they learn to deal with the rush of hormones that come with puberty. The primary concern we as parents need to focus on is making sure our teenagers do not start using sexuality to cope with negative feelings. The inability to manage emotions is the primary issue that leads to compulsive sexual behaviors and pornography use in adolescents. That is why we have emphasized teaching children how to manage emotions.

We want to help our teenage children become resilient in their emotional life. Emotional resilience means they do not feel threatened by negative emotions and that they feel confident in knowing what to do when strong feelings do come. That will take a few years but we have a few years to teach them.

We teach emotional resilience by discussing feelings frequently and modeling healthy ways to react to strong feelings. When we focus on helping them resolve the emotions they are experiencing they will find it much easier to manage their sexual feelings as well.

Parent-Child Activity: Option 1

Personalizing Parent-Child Check-ins

This is an exercise to do as a first step in doing parent-child check-ins with an adolescent child. You can personalize what you and your child will talk about in the coming months and perhaps years. Feel free to modify this to fit you and your child.

Instructions:

Find someplace private to talk and make sure it is not too late in the evening, when your child may be tired and cranky.

1. Tell them, "It will probably become more difficult to resist things like pornography because adults are attracted to sex and you are becoming an adult. I want to have more adult conversations with you so we can work on that together."

2. Say, "All adults have things we need to avoid that we sometimes have a hard time avoiding or feeling attracted to. One of the things I am working on is avoiding_____." (You as the parent must have something you are working on avoiding. It could be drinking, gossiping, or watching too much TV. However, many parents still struggle with wanting to look at porn from time to time. If this is true of you, the *best* thing is to be honest about that with your child. They need to know that it is a common adult experience to sometimes want to look at porn. The title of this book is "Honest Talk," so let's try to practice that.)

3. Ask your child, "Besides looking at pornography, what is something else you want to avoid doing that is related to sexuality that you think you might feel tempted to do?"

4. Share another thing you want to avoid that you sometimes feel tempted to do. It helps if it is related to sexuality, though it does not have to be.

5. You may decide to record the two things each of you have decided to try to avoid. That is up to you.

6. Now take turns trying to think of which two emotions or feelings are the hardest for you to deal with. Examples

might be feeling: not good enough, failure, left out, rejected, disrespected, and so on. Look at the feelings charts in Appendix A for ideas if you like.

7. Finally, each of you work together to help each other determine what you might do when something happens that creates the two feelings each of you just wrote down. Examples might be to call or text each other, talk to God about it, go on a walk, listen to positive or uplifting music, exercise, or do something you enjoy. Be specific. Come up with two ideas each.

8. Tell your child that you want to check in with them fairly often about these things you just shared. The point will be to ask if the negative emotions occurred recently and if either of you did the thing you had planned on doing to deal with that feeling. You will also share if you had trouble with the things you are avoiding.

9. Decide if you want to meet at a specific time, perhaps weekly, or just check in informally when you happen to be together or feel like you need to.

10. Try to make sure no more than a week goes by before your first check-in. You may decide you don't need to talk that often later, but it is important to check in fairly soon the first time.

Parent-Child Activity: Option 2

Determining Key Emotional Triggers

You may find that you or your teenager is making little traction in moving past the things you are trying to avoid. If this happens, it is possible that you have not yet identified the emotions that cause each of you the greatest discomfort. If you think this may be true, try this exercise.

Instructions:

1. Go over with your teenager the last three times they failed at avoiding something they want to avoid. Have them tell you what happened earlier that day and the two or three days prior.

2. See if they were experiencing any of these feelings leading up to the time they gave in to temptation:

disliked	disrespected	not given empathy
misunderstood	abandoned	not allowed to express myself
ridiculed	put in danger	not given physical affection
ignored	condemned	lied to repeatedly
disregarded	judged	mislead
rejected	made fun of	not fully known
left out	a failure	not fully loved
excluded	alone or lonely	

3. If so, make this feeling the new key emotion to pay attention to.

4. See if the two of you can come up with something they could do anytime they have this feeling that could help. It is quite possible that the best thing they can do is tell you immediately when they have this feeling again.

5. Over the next week, check in with your teenager daily to see if they are feeling this way again. Do not wait until your next regular check-in.

6. Do not try to "fix" their feeling; just let them talk about it to you. Share times you felt that way.

11

Cleansing Conversations for Older Children

You likely noticed that in the last chapter we included conversation topics that we had been putting under the "cleansing conversations" in past chapters. That is because our conversations about emotions and sexuality merge as children reach puberty. We no longer talk about them as discrete issues because they are not at this age. One affects the other.

As you may have noticed in the last chapter, another change in our conversations with teenage children is that we talk to them more like we talk to an adult. That means we ask their opinion more often and allow them to shape their journey to sexual wholeness rather than always telling them what to do. We also share more of our own journey, including struggles we still deal with, to raise them up to our level. The biggest deterrent to a teenager striving for sexual wholeness is to treat them like a child. The greatest motivator is to treat them more like an adult.

That said, there are a few topics we can add at this age we have not covered so far. These are topics you can weave in to your parent-child check-ins or make them separate conversations you have at appropriate times.

What Happens in the Mind

I have mentioned sexual fantasy a number of times already, but we should take time to better explain how to talk about fantasy. It is a mistake to focus on outward behavior and ignore what is happening inside the minds of our teenagers. In the case of masturbation, the physical act is typically less of a problem than what is happening inside the brain. Jesus addressed this very issue when He confronted religious people who looked very good on the outside:

> *Woe to you, scribes and Pharisees, hypocrites! For you clean the outside of the cup and of the dish, but inside they are full of robbery and self-indulgence. You blind Pharisee, first clean the inside of the cup and of the dish, so that the outside of it may become clean also.*

> *"Woe to you, scribes and Pharisees, hypocrites! For you are like whitewashed tombs which on the outside appear beautiful, but inside they are full of dead men's bones and all uncleanness. So you, too, outwardly appear righteous to men, but inwardly you are full of hypocrisy and lawlessness.*[66]
> —*Jesus*

Due to their new adult hormones, our teenagers will begin to have more difficulty getting a sexual thought out of their minds once it enters. They will get a lot more "dirt" thrown on them than before, and it will be harder to remove.

Remember our bath analogy—the process of cleansing has not changed. Cleansing conversations are the bath that washes away the misinformation they are subjected to. Teenagers will need more frequent conversations to talk through their feelings and all the sexual messages thrown at them, not less. And they will need deeper conversations to remove the more stubborn temptations.

Some teenagers will move comfortably into these deeper conversations because we have been talking about personal things with them for years. Others may demonstrate a new reluctance to be

---

[66] Matthew 23:25–28 (NASB)

open with us. In most cases we can work through this, once we prove again that we are safe to talk to.

Explaining the Harms of Sexual Fantasy

The best way to introduce this topic is to share your own story. Doing so lets your teenager know that you know what you're talking about from experience, that they are not weird or messed up if they have already experienced sexual fantasy, and that this is safe to discuss with you. It does not matter if you dealt well with sexual fantasy as a teen. It only matters that you understand what it is like to struggle with it.

A teenager may or may not understand what sexual fantasy is exactly. If you are not sure your teen understands, you can explain that sexual fantasy is anytime we imagine in our minds seeing another person naked, having sex with another person, or imagining any other sexual situation. Do not worry that you are putting an idea in your teenager's mind. That idea will get in their mind with no outside influence so we might as well be honest and admit it happens.

Help them see that sexual fantasy is not the best use of our sexuality. The Bible does talk about sexual fantasy and refers to it as lust. We see both examples of Godly examples vowing to avoid lust and warnings not to engage in it.

I made a covenant with my eyes
*not to look **lustfully** at a young woman*[67]
—Job

*But I tell you that anyone who looks at a woman **lustfully***
has already committed adultery with her in his heart.[68]
—Jesus

You might ask your teen why they think Jesus warned us not to engage in lust? God does not give us rules to make life miserable or no fun. Any warnings God gives are for very good reasons.

You might next share with your teen any negative consequences you have experienced yourself because of lust. That could be

---

[67] Job 31:1 (NIV) emphasis added
[68] Matthew 5:28 (NIV) emphasis added

consequences you experienced after engaging in sexual fantasy, consequences you experienced because of other's lust, or consequences you have observed in the greater community.

You can return to God's design for sex and discuss how sexual fantasy does not fit into that design. Sex is a bonding agent between husband and wife. Sexual energy toward another person who is not our spouse, even if only imagined, potentially weakens the bond we one day want with our spouse. Ask your teen what they think about this analogy. Does it make sense to them? Do they see harm in sexual fantasy and is this something they want to try to avoid? Allow them to answer honestly.

Avoiding Lust

We want to help our teenagers think through situations that they can avoid that may unnecessarily entice them toward lust. This is a skill they need to learn now that will benefit them the rest of their lives. The earlier they learn this practice the better.

Teenagers may not be fully aware of what situations will make them vulnerable to temptation. Teens often overestimate their ability with self-control. Teenagers may also be a little embarrassed to admit things they are already aware of that create temptation. To help with both of these problems, we share first.

We are adults with just as much possibility of engaging in sexual fantasy as our teenagers. We can be honest with our teenagers about any current steps we take as a matter of habit to avoid fueling lust in our own hearts. Are there places you don't go in order to avoid enticing lust? Are their movies or shows or websites that you make a habit of avoiding? Set an example by sharing what you have learned to do.

Then ask your teenager what they think they can do to avoid putting themselves in a situation that requires a lot of willpower to resist temptation. This is a conversation you should have more than once, even making goals to work toward.

But do not make this conversation about only your teen, make it about things you *both* can do to avoid lust. Treat your teenager as an equal in this area. Make this a journey you take together. Challenge each other and congratulate each other for wise choices. Doing so greatly improves the chances your teenager will take avoiding lust seriously.

We move away from sexual fantasy the same way we move away from pornography. We start by making sure we are not using fantasy as a way to avoid painful emotions. Unlike pornography, however, sexual fantasy does not require Internet access. A teenager, or adult for that matter, can enter the false intimacy of sexual fantasy any time, anywhere, in an instant. It requires more skill and practice to resist the temptation to fantasize than to resist finding a device to look up pornography.

One needed skill is to understand the difference between a God-designed sexual feeling, temptation to enter lust, and actually entering into lust. Many teens cannot decipher between these three feelings and may assume that any sexual feeling is lust and therefore sin. When they believe this, they may not even try to hit the pause button and move into lust when they did not start in lust. We will explain how to teach a teenager this skill next.

Biology, Temptation, & Lust

To a teenager with raging hormones, a God-designed sexual reaction can feel the same as sexual temptation and lust. God does not view them at all the same, and neither should we. We don't want our children to feel ashamed of the sexual feelings God gave them. We do want them to walk away from temptation, however.

To be honest, I'd never really thought about this distinction much until my thirteen-year-old son came to me with a confession. We had regular check-in meetings we called "accountability meetings." During one of those meetings, I could tell he looked uncomfortable. He then told me that he had "messed up" that week.

I asked him to explain and he said, *"I was in gym class, and this girl was wearing short-shorts, and . . . I messed up."*

I didn't understand what he meant so I asked for clarification.

He explained, *"Well, she was wearing short-shorts and I just wanted to look at her so bad, and I failed and I feel so horrible!"*

I was confused as to what he meant by "failed" so I asked him, *"You said you wanted to look at her; did you keep looking at her?"*

"No."

"Did you fantasize about her being naked?"

His eyes got wide, and he said he had not.

I asked, *"Did you masturbate at home thinking about her?"*

"No, nothing like that," he replied.

Then I finally realized what he was talking about. He had seen an attractive girl with most of her legs visible and had become sexually aroused. He apparently assumed that this meant that he had sinned. I had to smile at his misunderstanding.

I then explained to him that God designed us to have a strong physical reaction to seeing someone attractive. I told him all adults have a biological reaction to people we are attracted to, and that this is what he felt.

It was at that point that I realized my son needed to know the difference between a God-given biological reaction, temptation, and lust. It took us a while to get that all worked out, but the following is what we eventually came up with together.

Biological Reaction

Our teens likely know this, but it is good for parents to reassure them that it is normal and beyond their control to have a physical reaction to anything sexual and/or romantic. Adult bodies are designed to react instantly to any sight, sound, or touch that could be interpreted as sexual. In young teenagers these reactions are stronger and less controllable due to how unaccustomed their bodies are to adult hormones.

These biological reactions can include:

- increased heart rate
- sense of excitement
- blushing or flushing skin
- tingling sensations
- strong attraction
- physical arousal, such as erections in males

God created us to respond automatically and in a physical way to the opposite sex once we reach our teen years. These reactions do not occur because a teen decided they should happen, and they should not feel any sense of shame when it does happen. Our teenagers will have to be taught that this is normal and good, not a bad or sinful thing.

We can teach them that God intends for these reactions to happen to attract us to a future mate and, once we are married, to continually attract us to our spouses. These reactions will serve to bond us to our spouses. This is one part of the holiness of sex. It serves a holy purpose of continually drawing a man and wife together.

I told my son that it was good to see his body was working correctly. He was a little embarrassed, but seemed to take comfort in my assuring words.

Temptation

We use the word "temptation" to describe an internal desire to do something that we know we shouldn't do. After encountering a sexually charged event and experiencing a biological reaction, we can become tempted to act inappropriately. This usually starts with a lingering look at whomever we have encountered or continuing to play it over in our minds after we stop looking. The longer we keep looking or remembering what we encountered, the stronger the sense of temptation grows.

However, temptation is not a sin. Jesus was tempted in all things, which had to include sexual temptation.

> *For we do not have a high priest who is unable to empathize with our weaknesses, but we have one who has been tempted in every way, just as we are—yet He did not sin.*[69]
> *—Unknown New Testament Author*

Even as strong as sexual temptation feels, temptation is not a sin against God. Temptation does not harm us but is something all of us experience.

One of the best ways to help teenagers talk about temptation is to share times you were tempted. Notice that the Bible says Jesus can empathize with us *because* He was tempted. You can empathize with your teenager because you have been tempted. Your teenager needs to know this.

---

[69] Hebrews 4:15 (NIV)

We should keep in mind, however, that the more we focus on whatever is tempting us, the more likely it is that we will give in to it. Lingering on temptation is never a good idea. Telling someone about a temptation, like a teenager telling a parent, often helps the temptation go away. We don't call these "cleansing conversations" for nothing—they help wash away temptation, among other things.

Lust

Jesus categorized lust as sin when He said it was the same thing as adultery. Adultery is a sin forbidden in the Ten Commandments:

> *You shall not commit adultery*[70]
> *—The Prophet Moses*

Put in terms that a teenager can understand, lust is when we engage in sexual fantasy. That includes imagining someone being naked, imagining having sex with someone, or imagining watching others having sex. It also includes viewing pornography, watching any kind of media that, while not technically pornography, was designed to cause sexual arousal, and reading erotic stories.

Lust draws us away from real relationships and into isolation, and is therefore harmful. Lust reduces our emotional bond to real people, including our spouse or future spouse. Lust also erodes our bond with our heavenly Father, making us feel isolated and ashamed. God calls lust a sin and wants us to avoid it, because it will harm us.

Progression from a Reaction to Lust

The typical progression, when we let it proceed without caution, is to experience a biological reaction to something or someone we see; feel tempted to imagine sexual situations or perhaps go look at pornography; and finally give in and engage in sexual fantasy, pornography, and possibly masturbation. Of course, lust can also include engaging in physical sexual contact.

Reaction ➜ Temptation ➜ Lust

---

[70] Deuteronomy 5:18 (NASB)

When teenagers don't understand this distinction, it is easy for them to assume that when they feel aroused, they have already sinned. If they have already sinned, there is no distinction in their minds between a biological reaction, temptation, and lust. In such a case, a teenager sees no reason not to enter fantasy when he or she thinks they have already sinned. If there is no difference in their mind between feeling sexually excited and engaging in a sexual fantasy, there is no reason not to. Even if they do not move on to sexual fantasy, we still do not want them to feel shame for their body reacting the way God designed it to.

The good news is that teenagers don't have to let a biological reaction progress to lust. We can teach our children to look away, or even move away from something to which they feel a sudden, powerful attraction. They can tell us as soon as possible, perhaps via text, to get it off their chest. This helps wash any temptation away.

Of course, if we want our teenagers to do this, we need to model it for them. I texted my teenage son if I felt attracted to something or tempted. He needed to know this was an adult condition, not a teenage one. I had to show him what adults who are pursuing sexual wholeness do when they feel sexually tempted. We tell someone else whom we trust so that we do not continue.

I encourage you to teach this to your children when they reach puberty. Having this knowledge will reduce shame about how God made them and give them better understanding to resist temptation.

Relationships and Dating

We cannot ignore relationships and dating in our conversations with teenagers. If our teenagers are not dating, that does not mean we don't have to talk to them about sexuality and relationships. All teenagers need help creating guidelines that keep them safe.

Teenagers do not fully appreciate how heightened their sexual feelings are. They often do not believe they would ever do anything physically inappropriate with another person, but as parents we usually know better. Teenagers do not understand how powerful sexual feelings can be when they find themselves in a room alone with someone they feel attracted to. You may want to review chapter eight as a reminder of how teenage minds work. They often assume they have more control of themselves than they really do.

It is good to warn your teenage child how powerful these feelings can be. They may not believe you. You might share a story or two of when you were caught off guard at their age by how strong your feelings were. Then you should talk together about guidelines and expectations for relationships at their age. One of those should be to never be alone with someone of the opposite sex. Things can get carried away in such instances very quickly.

An Example

One mother shared this story with me that illustrates the point. Her teenage daughter had a boyfriend over and when the mother could not find them she walked by her daughter's room. Her daughter had left her door open but they were kissing and the mother recognized the passion between them. She told her daughter to stop and come back out.

Her daughter said, *"Mom, we were just kissing. It's no big deal!"*

The Mom replied, *"If it's no big deal, then why does your boyfriend have an erection?"*

Needless to say, the kissing stopped at that point. Teenagers really do not understand how strong their hormones are, and they need limits to keep them out of trouble.

Dating

One book cannot cover every parenting issue related to teaching children sexual wholeness. As such, and because there are several good books on deciding how to work with teenagers on dating, I will refer you to Appendix B to find resources on dating if you need those. There is a section on *Dating,* but there are also several books in the *Pursing Sexual Wholeness* category that speak to dating.

The other advice I would give is not to read up on the issue and then dictate to your child what you want them to do. That does not go over well and is in contradiction to the rest of the approach I have been teaching. If dating is just a list of rules, teenagers typically just break them and don't tell you.

Instead, discuss the topic together and try to come up with something you can both agree on. Perhaps you can get them to read one of the books on dating with you. It is okay to tell them that if they want to date, they need to get more information and you will do that with them. It is also okay to challenge our teenagers' rationale when we see that it is flawed. We can point out weaknesses in their arguments and ask questions like, "How does that fit into God's design for sex?"

Try not to let dating become a fight. Our relationship with our children is more important than how perfectly they walk toward sexual wholeness. Don't let dating become so divisive it damages your relationship with your teen.

Healthy Online Relationships

The main difference between online and face-to-face communication is that all people, adults and children, tend to act differently online than in real life. In online relationships, we typically try to portray who we want other people to imagine us as, not who we really are. This, in itself, is not particularly healthy. People tend to say things that do not fit their own moral code online; things they would never say face-to-face. As a result, many people tend to be far less healthy online than offline. It is very easy to develop a kind of split personality—our in-person self who is genuine and our online self who is not.

This does not mean we should forbid teenagers from using social media. Social Media and the Internet are not going away. We need to teach our children how to use these safely, because some day we won't be there with them to help. Start with one or two social media options, and for a while, follow what your child does closely. Allow your child to have more access when you feel they are ready.

Explain to your child that we need human interaction in order to have people to work through our emotions with. However, they need to know that social media is not a place to do this. Social media and online communication are not good places to work through hard feelings. Your teen needs lots of face-to-face interaction with their peers. Encourage this and even help them arrange time with friends if you need to. Perhaps suggest they spend as much time with friends face-to-face as online.

Talk about what you and they see on social media. Discuss whether these conversations reflect healthy or unhealthy views, not just of sex but life in general. Help children decide who to link to and when to cut someone off. Talk about times you decide to stop following someone on social media and why.

Don't allow children this age to take any Internet device to private places or behind closed doors. There are no good reasons for a child this new to hormones to have private access to anything online. Help your child out by removing the temptation to say or do inappropriate things online while unsupervised.

Use Internet safety software. Filtering is never enough as it's too easy to get around. Internet Accountability software, such as Covenant Eyes, will help you see what your child is doing online. Do this at least with the devices your family owns.

Finally, talk with other parents about what they do to help their kids learn to be safe online. We get good ideas and learn what not to do by talking with other parents. There is no reason you should be trying to navigate keeping your kids safe online alone.

Responding to Failure

It is inevitable that from time to time our teenagers will not live out sexually perfect lives. Even the best teenager can give in to sexual fantasy, look at pornography on purpose, and masturbate to fantasy or porn. They will fail to walk away when a friend is telling a sexual joke. They will develop crushes on boys or girls who would not make healthy boyfriends or girlfriends. They may give in and have some form of sexual contact, even if they have sworn to themselves they would not. It will help us if we prepare ourselves for the less-than-perfect sexuality our children are going to exhibit.

Perhaps it is helpful for us to remember that none of this surprises God. He knew everything our adolescents were going to do before they were even born. Still, He demonstrated unending love for them:

*"But God demonstrates his own love for us in this: While we
were still sinners, Christ died for us."*[71]
—*The Apostle Paul*

In the midst of our worst moment, God loved us this much. On
our teenager's worst day, God loves them this much. If God can love
our children this much, we can aspire to accept and love them in any
mess they create with their choices.

Parents Make Mistakes Too

I grew up in a rather rigid church. People were not particularly
open to sharing their failures with the church community. As a
result, by the time I was a teenager, I didn't think adult Christians
ever committed any form of sexual sin. That false belief only made
me feel worse as I struggled with my own sexual fantasy and
pornography use.

Now that I am an adult, I realize how inaccurate my teenage
view of Christian adults was. We all fall short in one way or another
in our sexuality. If our children do not already know this, they need
to know this by the time they are thirteen.

Another truth I have experienced is that when we begin helping
our children move toward sexual wholeness, it gets Satan's
attention. I found that when I started doing the things in this book
with my teen children, I began to experience stronger sexual
temptation than I had felt in years. I truly believe this was Satan
trying to make me stop helping my kids. Satan knew that if my wife
and I helped our teenagers in this way, it would cause them to
pursue God more strongly. Satan threw all kinds of sexual
temptations at us. Many other parents have shared similar stories
with me.

If you actually do any of the things mentioned in this book, it is
quite possible that you will be tempted or even falter in your own
sexual integrity in some way. Please do not let that scare you off. My
experience proves that when we lean into God, He turns around
what Satan would plan for evil to work for good.

---

[71] Romans 5:8 (NIV)

When Our Failures Help Our Children

When my son was fourteen, he started making real progress in resisting temptation, as he described in his story of walking home from school. Not long after that time, I experienced sexual temptation that was stronger than I'd felt in a very long time. I ended up giving into temptation and escaping into sexual fantasy for a couple of days.

I realized that if I was going to be honest with my son, I was going to have to tell him. I was very afraid he would consider me a failure and no longer want advice from me. My thoughts were, "What kind of example is a father who can't do what he's asking his son to do?" I somehow mustered up the courage to tell him that I had given in to sexual fantasy. I did add that I had already told my support network and was talking to God about it, but I was still afraid of what his reaction would be.

My son stopped moving, and I could tell he was thinking about something deeply. Then he let out a long sigh. Finally, he said, "I'm sure glad I'm not the only one." This was not the response I expected.

My son had just learned that his father knew very well the struggle he went through. Instead of making me less in my son's eyes, my confession made me greater. From that point on, my son became much more open with me, and even more willing to try suggestions I gave him. My failure resulted in greater sexual wholeness in my son. Of course, that is only possible when we are honest about our failures.

How honest you can be with your teenager about your own failures depends on what your spouse knows, if you are actively working on your issues, and how well your child can receive that information. If these are in place, such an admission can model for a teen what to do when they have a failure. Your failures do qualify you to mentor your child, but we need to be walking with God and our community toward health to be effective.

Parent-Child Activity: Option 1

Explain Lust to Your Teenager

If your child is at least thirteen, you may want to teach them to identify lust and how to tell the difference between it, a bodily reaction, and temptation.

Instructions:

1. Read the section, Biology ➜ Temptation ➜ Lust with your teenager. Do this aloud or silently one at a time.
2. Think of a time when you were a teenager and you felt a God-designed sexual reaction to something innocent. Share what the situation was in appropriate detail.
3. Ask your teenager if they have ever felt a reaction like that. You do not have to ask what they were reacting to unless they want to tell you.
4. Have a discussion about what each of you think God thinks of us when He sees us reacting like this. Perhaps share what you thought as a teenager and if you think differently now. Let your teenager process this and try to come up with how they think God views this.
5. If you feel comfortable and your teenager appears to be handling the conversation relatively well, share a time when you were their age and felt tempted to sexually or romantically fantasize about someone. You should add that temptation of this nature does not go away but is something all adults have to learn to deal with.
6. Ask them if they understand the difference between temptation and lust. You could ask them to explain the difference to you.
7. Have a discussion about what each of you thinks would be most helpful for you to do in order to avoid letting temptation turn into lust.
8. Read Hebrews 4:15 and Romans 5:8 together (they are also written out in this chapter). Talk about how that makes each of you feel.

Parent-Child Activity: Option 2

A First Discussion on Dating

You may or may not decide to use an additional resource to guide this conversation. If you feel comfortable discussing dating with what you already know, that is fine. Otherwise, consider one of these additional resources:

Younger Adolescents

- *Relationships: 11 Lessons to Give Kids a Greater Understanding of Biblical Sexuality* by Luke Gilkerson

Teenagers

- *Boundaries in Dating* by Dr. Henry Cloud
- *True Love Dates* by Debra Fileta

Teen Girls in Particular

- *No Trespassing: I'm God's Property* by Leah Holder

Instructions:

1. Purchase one of the books mentioned above if you want and read through that first.
2. If you like the book, select the portions you want your teenager to read and have them read that.
3. Go to chapter seven in this book and review the section *Teaching God's Design for Sex* with your teen.
4. Ask your teenager how dating fits in with God's design for sex. Give them plenty of time to think before giving their opinion.
5. Tell them your opinion as to how you see dating fits in with God's design for sex.
6. Have a discussion about how old a teenager should be as a minimum age to start dating.
7. Say, "Just because a person is old enough to date does not mean they should go look for someone to date. How should a person decide who to date?"
8. Ask, "What is the purpose of dating?"

9. If your teenager is not interested or old enough to date yet, you can end here.

Teens Preparing to Date

If your teen is old enough and wants to date, consider discussing the following as well:

10. Ask, "What does having a girlfriend/boyfriend mean to you? How are they different than other friends to you?"

11. Ask, "What would you want to do with a girlfriend/boyfriend that you do not do with other friends?"

12. Ask, "What guidelines can we set up that will keep this relationship safe and honoring God?"

13. Discuss dating guidelines and come up with a list. If the discussion becomes heated, pause and come back to it later, but do not allow dating until you come to consensus with your teen about dating.

14. Include what is happening in any dating relationship in your parent-child check-ins.

15. You can give consequences if your child violates the dating guidelines you agree on. It is fair to have your child gain your trust in order to have privileges like dating. However, if you are too strict with consequences be aware that your child may simply date behind your back in response.

16. When you feel it is appropriate you can share your story with dating and what you learned from the choices you made.

Parent-Child Activity: Option 3

When Someone Fails

When either you or your teenager fails to uphold the sexual standards you are aiming for, use the following exercise together.

Instructions:

Meet in a private place and read and do the following together.

- Everyone fails sometimes. Discuss what that means.
- Being honest means being open about failures, even small ones. Take a moment and be honest with each other about your recent failures, not hiding parts of your story you didn't want to reveal.
- Did you fail to do one of the things you have told each other you would do to help deal with emotions? Did you text or call or talk when you felt bad or were tempted? Are you doing the things that help prevent failure?
- Is it more important to focus on not doing things we vow not do to or to focus on doing the things that help us deal with sexual temptation? Discuss that question together.
- Failures are lessons. Ask each other the following so that you can learn from this failure:
  - What events led up to the failure?
  - What emotions led up to the failure?
  - Did you have a plan in place for that emotion? If not, what is one you can create?
  - What other things can we change to reduce future failures like this one?
  - If you have a plan and it isn't working, something needs to change. What are you willing to change, to become more successful in this area?
- Failure does not mean we cannot do better. What do you plan to do differently in the future?
- Failure does not cut us off from love. Assure each other that what has happened does not affect your love for each other.
- Read Romans 5:8 together. Thank God for loving you.

- Sexual mistakes do not define who we are. Your identity has not changed. Your value has not changed. Talk about what that means to you.

12

Concluding Thoughts

We have covered many topics and conversations you could have with your children. The last thing I want anyone to feel is overwhelmed after reading this book. Here are some thoughts to help avoid that pitfall.

Focus on Where Your Child Is Now

If your child is six, you don't need to worry about addressing issues surrounding puberty yet. Put those chapters aside and focus on what your young child needs right now. You can get the book out again when they reach age nine or so to prepare.

If your child is thirteen, you should review the information presented for younger children, but put your larger focus on the information in Chapters eight and beyond. Glance through the earlier chapters, but don't try to start from the beginning and race through several years of conversations in one year to get your child caught up.

If you have children who fall into different age groups in this book, you may need to start at different places with each child. Or you may decide that your younger child is ready for an older conversation, or that an older child needs to review an activity for younger children. What an individual child needs most is not always related to age. You know your child better than anyone, so feel free to do what feels right for your child.

Start with Emotions

No matter how urgent addressing an issue of sexuality may feel, we need to start with emotional awareness. Helping children understand what they are feeling, why they are feeling it, and how to best resolve those emotions is critical to sexual wholeness.

Do not expect your children to understand their feelings quickly. Some children may pick up on their emotional state easily, but many will need a lot of time practicing. Make talking about feelings part of daily life in your family. You will do your child an enormous favor.

One Thing at a Time

None of us do well working on multiple issues at once. Children are no different. Your children need to practice one skill until they are successful, before adding another area on which to focus. After starting with an exercise with emotions, determine your child's next greatest need and add conversations around that. Use this book as a tool to look up how to talk about each issue, as you add it to your cleansing conversations with your children.

Cleansing Conversations

Have cleansing conversations often, and more frequently as children get older. Become the person your child feels most comfortable bringing questions about sexuality to. This book is a guide to conversations, not a regimen. Be sensitive to your child and have conversations around what they are being exposed to and the questions they have. You can add other conversations described in this book after those are dealt with.

Remember that these are conversations, not just teaching. Teaching does not cleanse; it informs. Cleansing comes from a two-way discussion with our children, to reconcile what they are seeing in the world around them with the truth of holy sexuality that God created.

Set a Date to Discuss Difficult Topics

Most of us put off topics we are afraid to discuss. When it comes to discussing the topics you have the greatest fear of, you will very likely need to plan ahead and set a date for them to occur. Plan where the best location would be to have a private discussion without distraction, and put a date on the calendar that your child is aware of. Remember that deep conversations often don't go well in the evening, when everyone is tired.

Honest conversations about sex become possible when we take it one step at a time and when we become proactive with our efforts. We succeed not because we are particularly eloquent during one discussion, but because we keep the conversation going.

Recognize Signs of Abuse

I would be remiss not to acknowledge the reality of sexual abuse in the world and how that affects honest talk about sex with our children. A parent may discover that a child has experienced some form of sexual abuse during discussions with them. A parent may notice behaviors that may indicate the child has experienced abuse. In either case, a professional should be immediately contacted for help.

Historical statistics in this country indicate that 1 in 4 girls and 1 in 6 boys are sexually abused before the age of eighteen.[72] Possible sings of abuse include a child showing unusual interest in or obsession with pornography, masturbation, or sexual experimentation with others. Sexually abused children often become more isolated and quiet than before.

These behaviors alone do not mean that a child has necessarily been abused. A child today can exhibit these sexual behaviors due to the influence of the sex-infatuated society surrounding them.

---

[72] National Association of Adult Survivors of Child Abuse, Retrieved from naasce.org, (2011)

Counselors who work with children have told me that children exposed to a significant amount of Internet pornography exhibit the same symptoms as a child who was sexually abused. In other words, the kind of pornography that exists today can itself abuse children exposed to it.

Please visit http://downloads.purelifeacademy.org and download the document, *Guide to Helping Sexually Abused Kids*, if you believe or know that your child has experienced sexual abuse.

Children Who Need More Help

Sometimes a parent tries everything in this and other books and their child seems to continue to be drawn into unhealthy sexual behaviors. When a parent is sure that abuse is not the problem, it can be confusing to know what to do. There is no shame in needing a little extra help as a parent.

Sometimes the parent simply needs a little help communicating effectively with their unique child. Other times there may be tools not mentioned in this book that are all a parent needs to make progress. Other times a child is simply more defiant by nature than the average child and a parent needs help knowing how best to respond.

There are many counselors, coaches, and even other parents who can provide help and insight into how to proceed in these circumstances. Ask people you trust what resources are in your area that could help you work through difficult situations. You can also get referrals and recommendations at contact@bebroken.com.

You Can Do This

I want to personally thank you for investing your time to improve your skills in talking with your children about sex. There is a step of courage taken when a parent buys a book like this. I want to end by encouraging you. There may be times your child is uncooperative or seems to be going backward and you wonder if you can really do this. I am convinced you can.

The Right Home

Your children are in the right home. Your family may face unusual challenges that are not addressed in this book. You may feel that your family is not cohesive enough to try all these steps. That does not mean you cannot take *some* steps to help your children. It could be that some of the ideas presented are not a good match for your home, and that is okay. Use the ideas that could work with your family. I am not trying to help you have a perfect child, because no such child exists. The goal of this book is to help you move your child a little closer to sexual wholeness, and that is possible in your home.

The Right Parent

You are the right parent to help your children. You may not feel prepared, but neither did my wife and I at first. You may believe that your child is not interested in talking with you about emotions and sex. I have found that most children will talk with their parents once the parent proves that he or she is safe. We do that by telling our stories first, which you can do. You also have many more tools than you did before. You have enough to start the conversation.

It's Not Too Hard

Guiding your children toward sexual wholeness is not too hard for you to do. Every parent can do something mentioned in this book. Pick something you feel more comfortable with and start with that. Then add more as you feel more at ease. Our goal as parents is progress, not perfection, and you can help your child make progress. Talk with other parents to gain their insights as well as support, as you try to talk with your children. No one said you had to do this alone, and you should not try to.

My wife and I did not feel prepared when we started talking with our children about sexuality. It was awkward at first, but more for us than for our children. We made lots of mistakes along the way, but our children forgave us. Our children were in no way perfect either, but they knew we cared about them and always came back when they strayed. God blessed our imperfect efforts, and He will bless yours as well.

Final Parent Exercise

Putting Your Plan Together

1. If you have children age 8 or younger, check the boxes of any of the following you have already begun to do:
    - ☐ Read books and pointed out emotions, used a feelings chart, or discussed emotions in the family
    - ☐ Taught them to identify feelings beyond, "mad, sad, and happy."
    - ☐ Answered your child's questions about sex
    - ☐ Discussed personal boundaries and modesty
    - ☐ Hug and hold them often
    - ☐ Explained at a basic level what pornography is
    - ☐ Gave them a plan of what to do when they encounter pornography
    - ☐ Explained the basics of what sex is

2. Select ONE next step you want to take if you have a child under age 8. Put a note on your calendar when you can start.

3. If you have children between the ages of 9 and 12, check the boxes of any of the following you have already begun to do:
    - ☐ Worked to help child find causes of their emotions
    - ☐ Talked some about what to do when a child has a painful emotion or feeling
    - ☐ Allow children to talk about how they feel instead of shutting them down
    - ☐ Explained fully what sex is
    - ☐ Discussed how sex is holy, sacred, good, from God and it binds us together emotionally
    - ☐ Told your story about your initial experiences with pornography
    - ☐ Explained how modern pornography is harmful
    - ☐ Ask if they have been exposed to pornography

- [ ] Review plans of what to do when exposed to pornography
- [ ] Taken steps to make electronic devices safer for your children
- [ ] Affirmed children as good examples of male or female
- [ ] Explained the child's identity in Christ
- [ ] Discussed peer pressure and how to handle it
- [ ] Shared your stories of peer pressure
- [ ] Shared how hormones will affect emotions and sexual feelings
- [ ] Shared how body growth will decrease willpower and how that affects thinking
- [ ] Share how changes in the feeling brain affect attraction to novelty and risk
- [ ] Share how changes in the thinking brain lag behind other changes and how that affects decision making
- [ ] Told your story about experiencing all these changes that come with puberty
- [ ] Discussed ways you and your child can compensate for these changes when they reach puberty

4. Select ONE next step you can take with a child between the ages of 9 and 12. Put a note on your calendar when you can start this.

5. If you have children between the ages of 13 and 18, check the boxes of any of the following you have already begun to do:

- [ ] Talked about masturbation and how it relates to emotions
- [ ] Discussed wet dreams with boys
- [ ] Started doing parent-child check-ins
- [ ] Share emotions regularly within the family
- [ ] Helped child connect feelings to the event that caused them
- [ ] Taught that it is okay to have negative emotions

- [ ] You know what your child's greatest weakness is emotionally (which emotions are most likely to cause them to want to escape)
- [ ] You have discussed means to deal with those emotions rather than escape
- [ ] Discussed sexual fantasy and how it is harmful
- [ ] Discussed the difference between biology → temptation → lust
- [ ] Discussed healthy relationships and dating
- [ ] Discussed healthy online relationships
- [ ] Been honest with your child about a time you have failed

6. Select ONE next step you can take with a child between the ages of 13 and 18. Put a note on your calendar when you can start this.

For all parents

7. How often to you want to discuss emotions with your children from now on?

8. What are you currently doing to address media safety in your home?

9. Is there anything you can do to improve media safety in your home?

10. What are you doing or could you change to facilitate more face-to-face interaction at home or between your child and their peers?

11. What can you do to encourage your children to spend more time interacting with peers face-to-face than interacting online?

12. What can you say or do with your children to affirm them in their maleness or femaleness?

13. What part of your story that your child does not know might be the best to share with them next?

14. What other parent(s) do you know who you might be able to discuss how your parenting is going with?

Appendix A
Feelings Charts

Girls' Feelings Chart

Exhausted	Confused	Ecstatic	Guilty	Suspicious
Angry	Hysterical	Frustrated	Sad	Confident
Embarrassed	Happy	Mischievous	Disgusted	Frightened
Enraged	Ashamed	Cautious	Smug	Depressed
Overwhelmed	Hopeful	Lonely	Loved	Jealous
Bored	Surprised	Anxious	Shocked	Shy

Boy's Feelings Chart

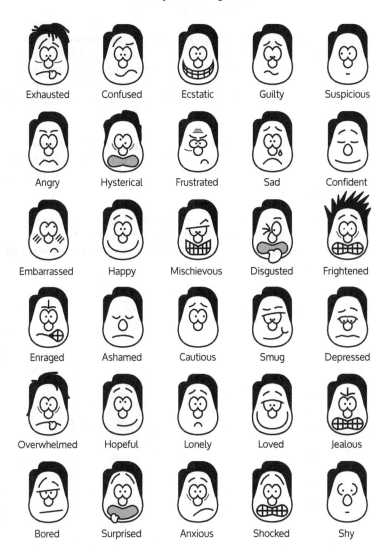

Exhausted	Confused	Ecstatic	Guilty	Suspicious
Angry	Hysterical	Frustrated	Sad	Confident
Embarrassed	Happy	Mischievous	Disgusted	Frightened
Enraged	Ashamed	Cautious	Smug	Depressed
Overwhelmed	Hopeful	Lonely	Loved	Jealous
Bored	Surprised	Anxious	Shocked	Shy

Download a printable version or a version without names at:
downloads.purelifeacademy.org

Complex Feelings

Mad, Sad, and Glad (or happy) are considered surface feelings as they do not tell us much about what is going on inside us. In the chart below, feelings directly under the labels mad, sad, and glad will be expressed with those three surface feelings. There are two other columns between the surface feelings. These may be outwardly expressed in two ways, depending on the child.

For example, a child who is frustrated that something is not working may appear mad or sad. A child who is feeling empathy for someone else may act happy or may act sad if they are internalizing the feelings of the other person.

These are not all the feelings a child might have but they do represent a good sample. Start by identifying which of the three surface feelings your child is experiencing then work down to select a more descriptive feeling.

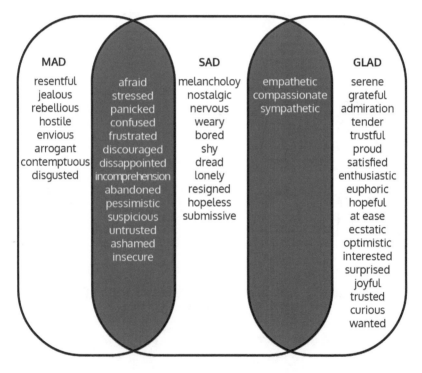

MAD		SAD		GLAD
resentful	afraid	melancholoy	empathetic	serene
jealous	stressed	nostalgic	compassionate	grateful
rebellious	panicked	nervous	sympathetic	admiration
hostile	confused	weary		tender
envious	frustrated	bored		trustful
arrogant	discouraged	shy		proud
contemptuous	dissappointed	dread		satisfied
disgusted	incomprehension	lonely		enthusiastic
	abandoned	resigned		euphoric
	pessimistic	hopeless		hopeful
	suspicious	submissive		at ease
	untrusted			ecstatic
	ashamed			optimistic
	insecure			interested
				surprised
				joyful
				trusted
				curious
				wanted

Appendix B
Additional Resources

The following are just a few additional resources you might want to consider to guide your conversations with your children. I do not necessarily agree with every point in all of these resources but they all contain information I think is valuable to any parent.

Teaching Emotions & Feelings

- *MySELF: I Have Feelings,* by Multiple Authors. A set of six books for children ages 3 and up to help children build emotional intelligence with prompts for real world discussions.
- *A Child's Book of Virtues* by William Bennett. Common childhood stories parents can use to point out emotional reactions and discuss how we react to our feelings.
- *A Child's Book of Heroes* by William Bennett. Common childhood stories parents can use to point out emotional reactions and discuss how we react to our feelings.
- *Parenting from the Inside Out,* by Daniel Siegel MD & Mary Hartzell. A parenting overview focusing on an emotional awareness approach to parenting.
- *Safe House: How Emotional Safety Is the Key to Raising Kids Who Live, Love, and Lead Well,* by Joshua Straub. Using emotional safety as a foundation from which you parent.
- *The 5 Love Languages of Teenagers,* by Gary Champan. Helps parents identify and appropriately communicate in their teen's love language, another form of emotional communication.

Body & Development

- *My Body is a Gift from God,* by Sherie Adams, MFT. Very appropriate book for young children to introduce topics like modesty.
- *God's Design for Sex (Books 1 & 2),* by Stan & Brenna Jones. These books are purchased in a set of four, but the first two: *The Story of Me, Before I was Born,* are mostly about our bodies and are appropriate for younger children.
- *Raising Body Confident Daughters: 8 Conversations to Have With Your Tween,* by Danna Gresh. An easy-to-use mom's planning guide to build your mom-daughter connection..
- *It's Great to be a Girl,* by Danna Gresh. A Biblically focused book to help girls learn about their changing bodies and God's design for them in a positive light.
- *It's Great to be a Guy,* by Jarrod Sechler. A Biblically focused book to help boys learn about their changing bodies and God's design for them in a positive light.

- *The Ultimate Guys' Body Book: Not-So-Stupid Questions About Your Body,* by Walt Larimore, MD. A resource to help start and guide discussions about sexual development in boys.
- *The Ultimate Girls' Body Book: Not-So-Silly Questions About Your Body,* by by Walt Larimore, MD. A resource to help start and guide discussions about sexual development in girls.
- *Changes: 7 Biblical Lessons to Make Sense of Puberty,* by Luke Gilkerson. This devotional is a series of 7 parent-child Bible studies designed to help a pre-teen child (8 to 12 years old) understand the changes he or she can anticipate—both from a biological and Biblical point of view.
- *Preparing for Adolescence: How to Survive the Coming Years of Change,* by Dr. James Dobson. This is an older, classic piece but still as true today as when it was written. Helps children prepare for the emotional changes they will experience at puberty, as well as physical changes.

Personal Safety & Boundaries

- *Say "NO!" and TELL! Daxton's Creative View of Personal Safety for Boys,* by Kimberly Perry. A book to read with boys to teach them personal safety and abuse prevention. Creative story format that balances innocence and wisdom.
- *Say "NO! and TELL!: Maisie's Creative View of Personal Safety for Girls,* by Kimberly Perry. A book to read with girls to teach them personal safety and abuse prevention. Creative story format that balances innocence and wisdom.
- *Say "NO!" and TELL!: Training Grown-ups in Boundaries and Personal Safety for Kids,* by Kimberly Perry. Training workbook for parents to help prevent the sexual abuse of children.

God's Design for Sex

- *Next Talk,* by Mandy Majors. This book actually covers many topics and is very good at illustrating how to have sensitive conversations with your children. Demonstrates how to have discussions about sex, pornography, trading nude photos, homosexuality, and many more subjects.
- *The Talk: 7 Lessons to Introduce Your Child to Biblical Sexuality,* by Luke Gilkerson. *The Talk* is a series of seven studies, all anchored in the Scriptures, that helps parents to talk meaningfully with children about sexuality. *The Talk* was written for parents to read with children ages 6-10 years old.
- *God's Design for Sex, (Books 1-4),* by Stan and Brenna Jones. Stan and Brenna's books include *The Story of Me,*

Before I Was Born, Facing the Facts, and *What's the Big Deal?* These books help parents educate children about healthy sexuality and intimacy at appropriate ages.

- *Guide to Talking with Your Kids about Sex,* by Focus on the Family. A comprehensive guide for parents on talking to their children about sex and sexuality.
- *Father + Son: Talk About Sex,* by Freedom Begins Here. This is a DVD set purchased online from FreedomBeginsHere.com. For dads who want help starting conversations about sex with near-pubescent boys. Watch this DVD with your son and it will do the work for you of starting the conversation.

Adolescents Pursuing Sexual Wholeness

- *Father-Son Accountability: Integrity Through Relationship,* by John Fort & Lucas Fort. A book for fathers and sons ages 12 and up to read together. Acts as a companion book to *Honest Talk* by explaining parent-child accountability in greater detail.
- *Pure Teens,* by Dr. John Thornington. Pure Teens is a valuable, practical resource for every Christian teen about relationships and sex—and why they are such a big deal to God.
- *No Trespassing: I'm God's Property,* by Leah Holder. Not all parents understand the sexual pressures teen girls are faced with today. Leah, age 19 at the time of writing, presents truths and personal testimonies regarding how we can be sexually pure within this sex-crazy world.
- *Choosing to Wait,* by Laura Gallier. A Parent's Guide to Inspiring Abstinence gives readers a refreshing alternative approach for rearing sexually pure kids. The book contains discussion questions and discussion road maps, which equip parents to initiate and facilitate quality conversations with their kids about the subject matter from each chapter.
- *Every Young Man's Battle,* by Stephen Arterburn & Fred Stoeker. A book for fathers and sons to read together. Helps bring up issues that boys will face and plan ahead to be more successful.
- *Every Young Woman's Battle,* by Shannon Ethridge & Stephen Arterburn. A book for mothers and daughters to read together. Helps bring up issues that girls will face and plan ahead to be more successful.
- *What are You Waiting For?* by Danna Gresh. A book for teen girls that discusses sex and relationships from a Biblical perspective.

Relationships & Dating

- *Relationships: 11 Lessons to Give Kids a Greater Understanding of Biblical Sexuality,* by Luke Gilkerson. A parental guide to teach kids how to relate to opposite sex friends and steward their sexuality in a godly way.
- *Boundaries in Dating,* by Dr. Henry Cloud. Specifically designed to help teens and young singles work through boundaries in dating.
- *True Love Dates,* by Debra Fileta. Insights from the expertise of a professional counselor to help teens learn how to use dating as a way to find real love.

Addressing Pornography

- *Good Pictures/Bad Pictures Jr,.* by Kristen A. Jensen. A great first book for children ages 3-6. The work has been done for you in knowing what to say.
- *Good Pictures/Bad Pictures,* by Kristen A. Jensen and Dr. Gail Poyner . The current best resource for explaining how pornography attracts us and how to resist it, for ages 6-9.
- *How to Talk to Your Kids about Pornography,* by Educate and Empower Kids. This resource is better to use with older children and teens as it goes into much more detail as to how pornography negatively affects us.
- *Brain, Heart, World,* by Fight the New Drug. A phenomenal set of three video documentaries on the affects of pornography on the brain and steps teens can take if they feel compelled to view pornography. Available at: brainheartworld.org

Other Resources for Parents

- *CovenantEyes.com.* Get regular posts on parenting for sexual purity. Go to the BLOG page and select "Protect Your Kids." Covenant Eyes also has several free eBooks to help parents discuss sexuality and online safety with kids.
- *ProtectYoungMinds.org.* This website ONLY focuses on helping children resist pornography and has all kinds of great ideas.
- *imdb.com.* It is a good idea to pre-screen movies before letting your children see them. This is an effective and reliable site to help you can find a detailed review of every single potentially inappropriate word and scene that a movie has.

Appendix C
Parent-Child Activities
Repeated

Emotional Awareness for Young Kids: Option 1

I Had That Feeling Once

Tell your children you are reading this book, and that it gave you an assignment you would like their help with. You can do this with any child age four and up.

Instructions:

1. Turn to the feelings charts in Appendix A and show them to your children.
2. Tell them your assignment is to pick a feeling and ask everyone in the family to share a time they felt that way.
3. Let one of the children pick a feeling
4. You go first, sharing a time when you felt that way and how you reacted.
5. Let each other members of the family do the same.

Exhausted	Confused	Ecstatic	Guilty	Suspicious
Angry	Hysterical	Frustrated	Sad	Confident
Embarrassed	Happy	Mischievous	Disgusted	Frightened
Enraged	Ashamed	Cautious	Smug	Depressed
Overwhelmed	Hopeful	Lonely	Loved	Jealous
Bored	Surprised	Anxious	Shocked	Shy

Emotional Awareness for Young Kids: Option 2

Name That Feeling

Tell your children you are reading this book, and that it gave you an assignment you would like their help with. You can do this with any child age four and up.

Instructions:

1. Go to http://downloads.purelifeacademy.org and download either the boy or girl faces chart. These are the ones with no names of feelings.
2. Print the chart.
3. Cut up the chart so that each face is a separate piece of paper. We will call each piece of paper a card.
4. Put all the "cards" in a hat, basket, or bowl.
5. Have a child draw a card, and then try to name the feeling the face is showing.
6. Have the person who drew the card tell a time when they felt that way.
7. Move on to the next person.

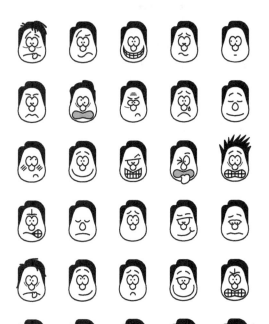

NOTE: You can start with only the easier emotions for younger children. You will know best which emotions your children will be familiar with.

It doesn't matter if the emotion a child names is exactly correct, as long as it makes sense compared to the face on the card.

Cleansing Conversations for Young Kids: Option 1

Prepare your child to know what to do when they encounter pornography

Purchase a book to guide a conversation between you and your child about the reality of pornography, why it is harmful, and what they should do if they ever see it.

The best book to choose depends on the age of your child. The following are some recommendations:

- **Ages 6 and under**: *Good Pictures/Bad Pictures Jr.*, by Kristen Jensen

- **Ages 7-12**: *Good Pictures/Bad Pictures*, by Kristen Jensen

- **Ages 12 and up**: *How to Talk to Your Kids About Pornography*, by Educate & Empower Kids

When you order the book, estimate when it will arrive. Mark a date on your calendar when you plan to read the book with your child, selecting a date after the book should arrive.

Alternate Idea: Use a Resource to Start Conversation about Sex.

You could use the same idea to go through a resource together about sex. For resources on teaching appropriate information to your child about sex, see Appendix B and look for book and DVD resources listed under *God's Design for Sex*. Select one that matches the age of your child and the kinds of topics you want to teach now.

Cleansing Conversations for Young Kids: Option 2

Find out what questions your child has about sex.

This is a good idea if your child is between ages eight and twelve. This is not a time where you teach new information but a time to answer questions.

Here is one way this could work. One parent take one child on an outing. This could be the parent that the child seems to bring questions to the most or the parent of the same gender of the child.

The outing could be a short hike, a place that child likes to eat, a fishing trip, or to toss a ball around.

> **Parent Tip:** It is often easier for a child to talk about sex when they do not have to look directly at the parent. If you are on a hike or fishing, this works well because we do not typically face each other doing those things. If you take the child out to eat or anything that causes you to be face-to-face, you might have the conversation in the car or walk on the way to or from the place you are going.

When you are ready, ask the child the following. Change the wording to match how you normally talk.

1. Do you ever hear kids talking about sex?
2. What do they say?
3. I want you to know that you can ask me anything, even questions about sex or words you think might have something to do with sex.
4. When I was your age this is a question about sex I did not know the answer to (share the question but not the answer).
5. Do you have any questions I could help you with?

It is okay if your child does not have any questions. You have let them know that it is okay to ask you about sex. You have also demonstrated that you know what it is like to have questions about sex at their age. This is enough even if they ask you no questions.

If they do have questions about sex, answer them but do not go into a long discussion unless your child seems really interested. We do not want them to think that every question they ask about sex will turn into a lecture. Do your best to make this a positive experience.

Emotional Awareness for Middle Kids: Option 1

Helping a Child Clarify an Emotion

Depending on the age of your child, this may be a good exercise. It will require you to watch your child carefully this week and look for an opportunity. This is a teachable moment exercise, not something you can mark on your calendar to do.

Instructions:

1. Watch your child this week and observe times when he or she seems to be mad, sad, or happy.
2. When you see one of these emotions come to the surface, stop what you are doing.
3. Sit down with him or her and ask how he or she is feeling. If they say, "mad, sad, or happy" do not try to clarify that feeling further yet.
4. Ask why they think they feel this way—that is, what happened to cause him or her to feel like this. Work with them to find the cause of their feeling.
5. If they still cannot identify a feeling beyond, "mad, sad, or happy" go to Appendix A and look at the *Complex Feelings* chart. Work together to try to find a more specific word to describe what they are feeling. Remember, the feelings chart is only a partial list of feelings.
6. Think of a similar situation in your life when you felt the same feeling, and share that story with your child of what happened and how you felt.
7. If your child seems open to more discussion, ask them what are good things to do when they feel this way.
8. Share what you do when you feel this way.
9. Thank him or her for telling you their feelings.

Emotional Awareness for Middle Kids: Option 2

Model Clarifying Emotions

Depending on the age of your child, this may be a good exercise. The goal is for you to use your own story to illustrate how emotions work and how we can clarify what we are really feeling.

Instructions:

1. Think of a time when something happened that created a strong negative emotion in you.
2. If you were to categorize your general reaction, was it closer to mad, sad, or happy?
3. Determine what feeling or emotion most clearly describes how you felt when this event happened? Use the feelings chart in Appendix A if you need to.
4. Now prepare to share this with your child.
5. Pick a time to talk with your child when they are not too busy. Make sure they are not tired or sleepy first.
6. Sit down with them and tell them this is a homework assignment for a book you are reading that you need their help with.
7. Tell them about the event that happened.
8. Tell them if this made you feel generally mad, sad, or happy.
9. Then tell them how you figured out which deeper emotion you really felt: such as shame, failure, insulted, disrespected, or so on.
10. Then tell your assignment was to ask them to help you decide what would be a good way to deal with this feeling if it happens again. Point them away from any suggestion based on revenge or fixing the initial event.
11. Talk through a few possible things you could do next time.
12. If they seem open, ask if they have ever experienced something like what you experienced and felt.
13. Thank them for their help. Do not overdo trying to apply your situation to theirs. They can figure that out on their own, unless they specifically ask for your advice on something.

Cleansing Conversations for Middle Kids: Option 1

Explaining God's Purpose for Sex

If you think your child is old enough to know more than just the mechanics of sex, this might be your next conversation with them. Plan ahead and select a time when your child will not be distracted. You could even have this conversation while driving in the car. Or you could be seated somewhere and use the following as conversation notes.

Instructions:

1. Ask your child where sex came from. Ask them whose idea was sex in the first place. Guide the conversation to the conclusion that sex was God's idea.

2. Ask them if they have ever thought about sex being God's idea. Ask them what they think this must mean.

3. Ask them if they knew that God has another purpose for sex besides making babies. Tell them you would like to explain what that is.

4. Tell your child something to the effect of, "**God created sex just for husbands and wives to share.** He created us so that when we have sex, a chemical called 'oxytocin' is released in our brains. This happens to men and women. When that chemical is in our brain, it makes us feel strong attraction to the person we are with and it makes us feel emotionally close to them. **Sex creates the feeling of a special, very close bond with that person.**"

5. That may be all you need to say. If your child seems interested, you could continue: "God created sex to be good, and making a husband and wife want to stay together is a good thing. God did not make sex just to help us have babies but to help us want to stay together. Each time a husband and wife have sex they want to stay together more."

6. If they ask why some mothers and fathers do not stay together, you could say that sex helps us want to stay together, but sometimes other things happen that cause

people to want to separate. Or, if a person uses sex in a way that is not considerate, it can be hurtful instead of helpful.

Cleansing Conversations for Middle Kids: Option 2

Use Questions to Open Conversation

We covered several topics as part of the cleansing conversations you can have with your nine to twelve year old children. One of the best ways to get such a conversation started is to ask your children questions about what they are seeing and hearing. This takes the heat off them as you are not asking what they may have done on purpose that they are afraid you would be mad at them for. You can get to those questions later, but the following are questions that feel safer for children when you start conversations about sex.

Instructions:

Plan ahead and select a time when your child will not be distracted to have this discussion. It is okay to tell them you are setting aside a time to talk, or you can make it seem spontaneous. When the day and time arrive, look through the following and select **one question** to ask your child.

- I know kids your age look at pornography. Do you ever overhear kids talking about pornography?
- When I was your age, kids told each other jokes about sex. Do you ever hear kids telling jokes like that?
- Do you ever hear kids talking about sexual things?

If they answer "yes," to any of the above, you should ask:
- What kinds of things do they say?
- What do you think about what they are saying?
- What do you think about (whatever the topic was)?
- Do you have any questions for me about this?
- What do you think God would have us do?
- Why do you think God would have us do this?

NOTE: This should not be a conversation that you are trying to drive in any particular direction. The goal is to get your child to start sharing what they are experiencing in their world and thinking through what to do with what they are being exposed to. Let the

195

conversation go where it goes without trying too hard to force it to go where you think it should.

It is always good to share part of your own story if you feel it would be helpful at any point.

Preparing for Puberty: Option 1

Start a Conversation About Puberty

This activity is recommended for children who are approaching puberty or within the first two years of puberty. The goal is not to discuss everything in the preceding chapter but simply start the conversation in the easiest way possible. If you feel your child falls in this range, consider doing the following with them.

Instructions:
1. Arrange a time to talk with your child that is private and comfortable.
2. Ask your child, "What do you know about the changes that happen with puberty besides changes to your body?"
3. If they mention something about emotions, ask them to clarify what exactly changes related to emotions.
4. Explain to them if they do not know that the same chemicals that cause their bodies to change also cause their emotional reactions to become stronger. Clarify with this fictional example:

A (boy/girl) is eight years old and is told they can't go to a party. They feel disappointed and cry but the next day they forget what happened. At age fifteen the kid's parents use exactly the same words to explain they cannot go to a party they want to attend. This time the teenager yells at their parents, storms out of the room and slams their door. They stay mad at their parents and hardly talk to them for a week. Exactly the same thing happened but the feelings of disappointment and being left out were many times more powerful when the boy/girl was fifteen year old. This is what it looks like to have more powerful feelings after puberty. This fades through the teenage years and eventually returns to normal again.

5. Tell a story of when you reacted with extreme emotions as a teenager.
6. If your child has reached puberty, ask them if they have experienced this yet.
7. Talk about ways the two of you can get through times when they experience extreme emotions.

8.   Assure them you love them even if this happens.

Preparing for Puberty: Option 2

Explain Changes in the Brain

The extent your child may be interested in what is or will happen in their brain during puberty is something only you can guess at. If you think they are ready and potentially interested, use this page to teach your child what happens to the human brain between ages ten and twenty five.

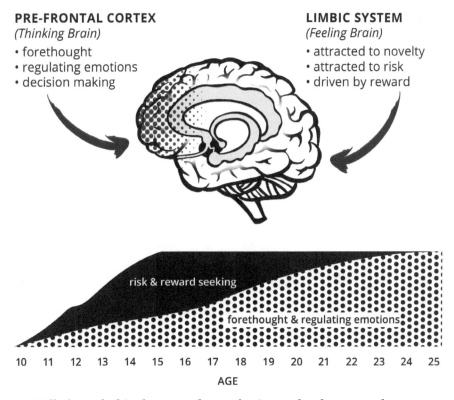

PRE-FRONTAL CORTEX
(Thinking Brain)
• forethought
• regulating emotions
• decision making

LIMBIC SYSTEM
(Feeling Brain)
• attracted to novelty
• attracted to risk
• driven by reward

risk & reward seeking

forethought & regulating emotions

10 11 12 13 14 15 16 17 18 19 20 21 22 23 24 25

AGE

Talk through this chart together, referring to the chapter to clear up any misunderstandings. Once you have done that, discuss the following questions together.

1. What does God have to do with all of this?
2. How could this 10-year period of change in how we think be used for good?
3. How might this make it more difficult to resist things like pornography during the teen years?

4. What are some ways you can work together to reduce the
    chances of making poor decisions about things like sex and
    pornography while this is happening?

Preparing for Puberty: Option 3

Teach Your Child About Willpower

This activity could be done with any child old enough to be interested. Read the following to your child and discuss the answers together.

Not many people use the word "willpower" correctly. Scientists use willpower to mean the amount of energy inside your body that is available to be used. Each of our bodies is able to carry a certain amount of willpower and no more. We don't really have a willpower "tank" like the picture, but this is an easy way to understand how it works.

Everything we do or think requires willpower or energy and everything we do or think uses up a little willpower. Here are a few things that need willpower to do and use it up when they happen:

- Opening your eyes
- Walking, running, climbing, or jumping
- Talking to your friend
- Deciding what to say
- Doing math
- Not reacting to someone who is being really annoying
- Growing taller

The harder it feels like a particular thing is to do, the more willpower it takes to do it. Feeling "hard to do" means you have to use a lot of willpower to do it. This includes trying to figure out schoolwork or making a choice between two things you really want.

This means every time you do or think anything, your willpower "tank" gets emptier. When your willpower tank is near empty, it becomes really hard to do anything, even thinking. We can tell when our willpower is getting low because we feel tired.

Willpower comes from food and sleep. We fill our tank back up by eating and sleeping. When we wake up and eat breakfast, our willpower tank is as full as it's going to get that day. If we didn't get enough sleep, that means we start with a tank that is not very full.

As the day goes on, we do eat some, but this only partially refills our tank. By the end of the day, we have very little willpower left, and it becomes hard to do or think as well as we can earlier in the day. This is what happens when you can't figure out how to do homework at night that you know should not be hard to figure out.

Questions to Discuss Together:
1. List five physical things and five thinking things that will be harder to do with a low willpower tank.
2. What are some ways a person might get into trouble during times they have low willpower?
3. A boy or girl is thirteen and starts to grow really fast, growing four inches in one year. Thinking about willpower, what would this do to him or her during that year?
4. A kid has decided they do not want to look at pornography because they know it is harmful. Can you describe a situation where this same kid finds it harder than normal to resist looking at pornography because of willpower?
5. We know that our willpower is usually lowest in the evenings. What are some things you and your family could put in place in the evenings so that you do not need as much willpower to make good decisions?
6. Each of you share a story of a time you think you had low willpower and how that turned out.

Addressing Masturbation: Option 1

A First Conversation

If your child is about a year away from puberty, or if they have already entered puberty and you've never talked about masturbation, you might consider this exercise. I would recommend the same gender parent as the child have the conversation, although that is not absolutely required.

Instructions:

Make a date with your child and go somewhere private to talk. This could be a car ride if you can't think of anywhere else to go. Then have the following conversation:

1. Say, "I want to talk to you about masturbation. I know this is an embarrassing topic, but we can discuss this like anything else."
2. Tell your child what your parents told you about masturbation, even if it was nothing. Tell them if this was helpful to you.
3. Tell your child questions or confusion you had about masturbation at their age, including what you imagined God thought about it.
4. Ask your child if they have heard other kids talk about masturbation and what they said if so.
5. Ask your child if they have any questions about masturbation. Answer their questions honestly.
6. If your child asks you if you ever masturbated be honest with them. Tell them how you learned about it and how old you were. Do not go into any detail but let them know this is something they can share with you by setting an example of sharing honestly with them.
7. If they volunteer that they have already masturbated you can go to the next exercise.
8. Tell them that you want to be where they learn correct information about sexuality, including masturbation. Tell them you want them to come to you if they ever have any questions at all about masturbation in the future.

9. This is a good place to end the conversation. You do not need to ask if they have masturbated or thought about it. This is just a first conversation.

Addressing Masturbation: Option 2

Responding to Masturbation

This is a conversation to consider having with a child the first time they tell you or you discover that they have engaged in masturbation.

Instructions:

Do not put this conversation off but get somewhere private and talk with them now. This is not a conversation to put on the calendar. Give your full and undivided attention to your child.

1. **Thank them for telling you.** If they told you, they just honored you with what is probably the most personal part of their life to date. Don't treat this like it is a huge deal but show respect for their honesty.

2. **Say, "You are not in trouble."** Whether your adolescent admitted to masturbation or was somehow caught you must assure them before saying anything else that they are not in trouble. Saying "You are not in trouble," removes shame from the equation. Shame will drive our children from God so it needs to be eliminated as soon as possible. You may want to hug your child or tell them you love them. They need to know we do not think less of them for masturbating.

3. **Tell your story.** If you have not done so yet, now is the time to tell your own story of the first time you masturbated. Keep it simple with no details but say how old you were and how you discovered it. Then tell them how you felt later about what you had done. Tell them how you thought God felt about you. Let your adolescent know you have been where they are. You are strengthening your relationship with them, which will make future conversations much easier.

4. **Tell them they are normal.** Make sure they understand that masturbation is something most adolescents do. It is good to explain that this is not God's ultimate plan for sexuality and this is something they will want to mature beyond doing. None-the-less, it is something almost all teens struggle to move beyond.

Addressing Masturbation: Option 3

Helping an Adolescent Mature

Here are some things you can do to help a teen that struggles with masturbation. When they admit to masturbating during a parent-child check-in:

1. **Find out if lust was involved.** Ask if they were looking at pornography or engaging in sexual fantasy. Check their understanding by asking how pornography and sexual fantasy are harmful to them and others. If you notice your child looking ashamed, remind them that we all fall short of our goals sometimes and learning to walk away from lust is a process.

2. **Find out if they were coping.** They may not remember, but ask what had been happening before this event. Were they worried about something? Had someone been unkind to them? If they were experiencing a negative emotion before they masturbated ask them what they could do next time instead to deal with that feeling.

3. **Is there a pattern developing?** Is there a day or time of day when masturbation occurs more often? What else is going on or was going on that may have been a contributing factor? What does this tell us about what might influence your adolescent to engage in masturbation? Is there something we can do to change the situation or the adolescent's response to it?

4. **Tips for bedtime.** If this happened at night, help them come up with ideas that could help them redirect their arousal before going to sleep. Ideas might include:
   - Allow positive music to play softly as they fall asleep
   - Pray and thank God for what they are grateful for
   - Recall fond memories of family or time with friends
   - Have them read a book until they are too sleepy to continue
   - Encourage them to sleep with their door open once they've changed for bedtime

Emotional Awareness for Older Kids: Option 1

Personalizing Parent-Child Check-ins

This is an exercise to do as a first step in doing parent-child check-ins with an adolescent child. You can personalize what you and your child will talk about in the coming months and perhaps years. Feel free to modify this to fit you and your child.

Instructions:

Find someplace private to talk and make sure it is not too late in the evening, when your child may be tired and cranky.

1. Tell them, "It will probably become more difficult to resist things like pornography because adults are attracted to sex and you are becoming an adult. I want to have more adult conversations with you so we can work on that together."

2. Say, "All adults have things we need to avoid that we sometimes have a hard time avoiding or feeling attracted to. One of the things I am working on is avoiding_____." (You as the parent must have something you are working on avoiding. It could be drinking, gossiping, or watching too much TV. However, many parents still struggle with wanting to look at porn from time to time. If this is true of you, the *best* thing is to be honest about that with your child. They need to know that it is a common adult experience to sometimes want to look at porn. The title of this book is "Honest Talk," so let's try to practice that.)

3. Ask your child, "Besides looking at pornography, what is something else you want to avoid doing that is related to sexuality that you think you might feel tempted to do?"

4. Share another thing you want to avoid that you sometimes feel tempted to do. It helps if it is related to sexuality, though it does not have to be.

5. You may decide to record the two things each of you have decided to try to avoid. That is up to you.

6. Now take turns trying to think of which two emotions or feelings are the hardest for you to deal with. Examples might be feeling: not good enough, failure, left out, rejected,

disrespected, and so on. Look at the feelings charts in Appendix A for ideas if you like.

7. Finally, each of you work together to help each other determine what you might do when something happens that creates the two feelings each of you just wrote down. Examples might be to call or text each other, talk to God about it, go on a walk, listen to positive or uplifting music, exercise, or do something you enjoy. Be specific. Come up with two ideas each.

8. Tell your child that you want to check in with them fairly often about these things you just shared. The point will be to ask if the negative emotions occurred recently and if either of you did the thing you had planned on doing to deal with that feeling. You will also share if you had trouble with the things you are avoiding.

9. Decide if you want to meet at a specific time, perhaps weekly, or just check in informally when you happen to be together or feel like you need to.

10. Try to make sure no more than a week goes by before your first check-in. You may decide you don't need to talk that often later, but it is important to check in fairly soon the first time.

Emotional Awareness for Older Kids: Option 2

Determining Key Emotional Triggers

You may find that you or your teenager is making little traction in moving past the things you are trying to avoid. If this happens, it is possible that you have not yet identified the emotions that cause each of you the greatest discomfort. If you think this may be true, try this exercise.

Instructions:

1. Go over with your teenager the last three times they failed at avoiding something they want to avoid. Have them tell you what happened earlier that day and the two or three days prior.

2. See if they were experiencing any of these feelings leading up to the time they gave in to temptation:

disliked	disrespected	not given empathy
misunderstood	abandoned	not allowed to express myself
ridiculed	put in danger	not given physical affection
ignored	condemned	lied to repeatedly
disregarded	judged	mislead
rejected	made fun of	not fully known
left out	a failure	not fully loved
excluded	alone or lonely	

3. If so, make this feeling the new key emotion to pay attention to.

4. See if the two of you can come up with something they could do anytime they have this feeling that could help. It is quite possible that the best thing they can do is tell you immediately when they have this feeling again.

5. Over the next week, check in with your teenager daily to see if they are feeling this way again. Do not wait until your next regular check-in.

6. Do not try to "fix" their feeling; just let them talk about it to you. Share times you felt that way.

Cleansing Conversations for Older Kids: Option 1

Explain Lust to Your Teenager

If your child is at least thirteen, you may want to teach them to identify lust and how to tell the difference between it, a bodily reaction, and temptation.

Instructions:

1. Read the section, Biology ➔ Temptation ➔ Lust with your teenager. Do this aloud or silently one at a time.
2. Think of a time when you were a teenager and you felt a God-designed sexual reaction to something innocent. Share what the situation was in appropriate detail.
3. Ask your teenager if they have ever felt a reaction like that. You do not have to ask what they were reacting to unless they want to tell you.
4. Have a discussion about what each of you think God thinks of us when He sees us reacting like this. Perhaps share what you thought as a teenager and if you think differently now. Let your teenager process this and try to come up with how they think God views this.
5. If you feel comfortable and your teenager appears to be handling the conversation relatively well, share a time when you were their age and felt tempted to sexually or romantically fantasize about someone. You should add that temptation of this nature does not go away but is something all adults have to learn to deal with.
6. Ask them if they understand the difference between temptation and lust. You could ask them to explain the difference to you.
7. Have a discussion about what each of you thinks would be most helpful for you to do in order to avoid letting temptation turn into lust.
8. Read Hebrews 4:15 and Romans 5:8 together (they are also written out in this chapter). Talk about how that makes each of you feel.

Cleansing Conversations for Older Kids: Option 2

A First Discussion on Dating

You may or may not decide to use an additional resource to guide this conversation. If you feel comfortable discussing dating with what you already know, that is fine. Otherwise, consider one of these additional resources:

Younger Adolescents
- Relationships: 11 Lessons to Give Kids a Greater Understanding of Biblical Sexuality by Luke Gilkerson

Teenagers
- Boundaries in Dating by Dr. Henry Cloud
- *True Love Dates* by Debra Fileta

Teen Girls in Particular
- No Trespassing: I'm God's Property by Leah Holder

Instructions:
1. Purchase one of the books mentioned above if you want and read through that first.
2. If you like the book, select the portions you want your teenager to read and have them read that.
3. Go to chapter seven in this book and review the section *Teaching God's Design for Sex* with your teen.
4. Ask your teenager how dating fits in with God's design for sex. Give them plenty of time to think before giving their opinion.
5. Tell them your opinion as to how you see dating fits in with God's design for sex.
6. Have a discussion about how old a teenager should be as a minimum age to start dating.
7. Say, "Just because a person is old enough to date does not mean they should go look for someone to date. How should a person decide who to date?"
8. Ask, "What is the purpose of dating?"

9. If your teenager is not interested or old enough to date yet, you can end here.

Teens Preparing to Date

If your teen is old enough and wants to date, consider discussing the following:

10. Ask, "What does having a girlfriend/boyfriend mean to you? How are they different than other friends to you?"

11. Ask, "What would you want to do with a girlfriend/boyfriend that you do not do with other friends?"

12. Ask, "What guidelines can we set up that will keep this relationship safe and honoring God?"

13. Discuss dating guidelines and come up with a list. If the discussion becomes heated, pause and come back to it later, but do not allow dating until you come to consensus with your teen about dating.

14. Include what is happening in any dating relationship in your parent-child check-ins.

15. You can give consequences if your child violates the dating guidelines you agree on. It is fair to have your child gain your trust in order to have privileges like dating. However, if you are too strict with consequences be aware that your child may simply date behind your back in response.

16. When you feel it is appropriate you can share your story with dating and what you learned from the choices you made.

Cleansing Conversations for Older Kids: Option 3

When Someone Fails

When either you or your teenager fails to uphold the sexual standards you are aiming for, use the following exercise together.

Instructions:

Meet in a private place and read and do the following together.

- Everyone fails sometimes. Discuss what that means.
- Being honest means being open about failures, even small ones. Take a moment and be honest with each other about your recent failures, not hiding parts of your story you didn't want to reveal.
- Did you fail to do one of the things you have told each other you would do to help deal with emotions? Did you text or call or talk when you felt bad or were tempted? Are you doing the things that help prevent failure?
- Is it more important to focus on not doing things we vow not do to or to focus on doing the things that help us deal with sexual temptation? Discuss that question together.
- Failures are lessons. Ask each other the following so that you can learn from this failure:
  - What events led up to the failure?
  - What emotions led up to the failure?
  - Did you have a plan in place for that emotion? If not, what is one you can create?
  - What other things can we change to reduce future failures like this one?
  - If you have a plan and it isn't working, something needs to change. What are you willing to change, to become more successful in this area?
- Failure does not mean we cannot do better. What do you plan to do differently in the future?
- Failure does not cut us off from love. Assure each other that what has happened does not affect your love for each other.
- Read Romans 5:8 together. Thank God for loving you.

- Sexual mistakes do not define who we are. Your identity has not changed. Your value has not changed. Talk about what that means to you.

About the Author

John Fort is the Director of Training for Be Broken, a national non-profit organization helping families move toward sexual wholeness. He has a master's degree in science education and taught middle and high school students for nine years before moving into adult education.

John has worked in full time ministry training leaders to assist families affected by sexual brokenness since 2008. He is also a regular blogger for ProtectYoungMinds.org and Covenant Eyes and has authored the books, *Father-Son Accountability: Integrity Through Relationship* and the fictional trilogy on integrity, *The Forbidden Scrolls*.

John has two adult children and lives with his wife in Oregon.

PURE LIFE
ACADEMY

MEN · WOMEN · PARENTS · YOUTH

online training for sexual wholeness
for the whole family

PureLifeAcademy.org

Made in United States
Troutdale, OR
04/10/2025

30511016R00126